FREEZER
COOKBOOK

CAVENDISH HOUSE

Contents

Written by Jill McWilliam
Illustrated by Colin Hawkins

Produced by
Faulkner/Marks Partnership
30/34 York Way, London N1 9AB
for Marshall Cavendish Books Limited

Published by
Marshall Cavendish Books Limited
58 Old Compton Street
LONDON W1V 5PA

© Marshall Cavendish Limited 1976, 1981

Printed in Hong Kong

First printed 1976 as *Eat Better, Eat Cheaper with your Freezer*
This volume printed 1981
ISBN 0 85685 960 5

Editor's note: Equivalents are given in the text for Imperial equivalents in ( ) brackets and American in [ ] brackets. All weight and measure equivalents are approximate.

Key to Symbols: The following guide to each recipe's freezer storage life is used throughout the book:
Up to 1 month Ⓛ
2-3 months ⓁⓁ
3-6 months ⓁⓁⓁ

Freeze and Save

A home freezer can save you money and be a great benefit and major asset in terms of convenience – if used in the correct way.

Unfortunately, a freezer does not come with a guarantee to save money – that is up to you. Careful shopping and sensible home-freezing can save at least 10 per cent of the weekly shopping budget. The convenience a freezer brings is often its greatest advantage. Apart from saving money, two important advantages are, less time spent on shopping and the facility to have a wide variety of food readily available.

This special cookbook has been produced to help you eat cheaper and eat better with your freezer. The first section explains exactly how to get the best out of the food from your freezer. The recipes have been specially chosen for freezing and there is a section on gardening for freezing.

Buying the freezer

The first thing to decide is where you can accommodate a freezer. Space is always the inhibiting factor, but do not make the common mistake of assuming that the kitchen is the only place to have your freezer. Obviously the kitchen is ideal from the convenience aspect, but generally kitchen space is limited. It is worth remembering that using a freezer efficiently means you should only need to go to it once a day or even less. So although convenient, kitchen location is not essential.

Location – points to remember
Kitchen
If sited next to a boiler or cooker, place a sheet of asbestos between the two appliances as extra insulation. The kitchen must be well ventilated especially when cooking.

Living area
Site away from radiators or other forms of direct heating if possible, otherwise use asbestos sheeting to insulate. Choose a quiet running machine and a wooden plinth may be required to place the freezer on to prevent damage to carpets.

Confined area (i.e. under stairs)
Ensure adequate ventilation either by means of an air brick or window.

Garage/out house
If these outside premises are damp, choose a machine which is not prone to condensation, otherwise rusting could occur. Condensation can be overcome by keeping a good coating of wax polish on the exterior and ensuring a good circulation of air, but rusting is inevitable eventually. A freezer that locks could be necessary but if these premises form an integral part of the house this problem should not occur.

Cellar
Ensure adequate ventilation particularly during the summer months. If prone to dampness take adequate precautions to prevent rusting.

Conservatory/glass outbuilding
If the freezer is to be subjected to sustained high temperatures, i.e. over 38°C (100°F) a fan cooled freezer is required.

Ideally during the summer months move the freezer to a cooler location, otherwise ensure plenty of ventilation by keeping doors and windows open.

Bedroom/landing
Choose a quiet running machine. Ensure the floor-boards can take the weight – particularly if an upright

model is being contemplated. When choosing a location the prime consideration should be the space available. It is difficult to ascertain in general terms the size of a freezer required by different sized families. It depends on several factors – the amount of catering and entertaining you do, the quantity of home freezing you do each month and the frequency of shopping trips and the quantities you wish to buy and store.

However, as a guide you can calculate 55 litres (2 cu ft) per person plus 55–110 litres (2–4 cu ft) extra. So a family of four would need 280–340 litres (10–12 cu ft) freezer. Ideally, though, it is much more sensible to buy the largest machine you can afford and accommodate as most freezer owners often complain about the fact that their freezer is too small. So in practical terms it is more beneficial to house the freezer where there is space to accommodate a larger one rather than site for convenience if it means a smaller freezer.

The temperature around should also be taken into account. High temperatures obviously increase running costs, whilst lower temperatures can have an adverse effect on the cabinet by slightly increasing the rate of deterioration.

Running costs

'How much does a freezer cost to run?' is like asking 'How long is a piece of string?' Many factors have an effect and these factors differ in each individual circumstance. The capacity, location and ambient temperature are the primary consideration, but other points must also be considered. Food is a much better insulator than air, so a well stocked freezer is more economical than one only a quarter full.

What shape

Having decided on location the choice between a chest and upright may have already been determined. Both types are designed to do an efficient job if sited correctly, but their various characteristics should be considered.

Chest	Upright
280–340 litres (10–12 cu ft)	280–340 litres (10–12 cu ft)
Initial outlay	
£100–£125 (1976 prices)	£150–£175 (1976 prices)
Storage	
9kg (20lbs) per 28 litres (1 cu ft)	7kg (15lbs) per 28 litres (1cu ft)
Ease of use	
Requires good organization and efficient stock rotation.	Easy access and stock rotation, sliding baskets and door space useful.
Defrosting	
Necessary once every 9–12 months. Simple, straightforward process.	Necessary once every 3–4 months. Rather time consuming and a little messy.
Space	
Large amount of floor space required.	Small amount of space required, usually 60cm (2 ft) square.
Running costs	
Economical	Average

Other features to look for

Worktop	– Useful in kitchen location
Lock	– Important in outside premises
Castors	– Provides easy movement for cleaning
Interior light	– Only necessary if sited in unlit location
Baskets	– Hanging and sliding baskets facilitate easy access and stock rotation
Adjustable feet	– Useful if siting on an uneven floor
Control panel	– Three light system is the most efficient
	Red – Warning
	Green – Power
	Amber – Fast Freeze
Adjustable thermostat	– Ensures a stable cabinet temperature and keeps running costs to a minimum

There really is not very much to choose between the two shapes. Perhaps the upright freezers look more attractive and are slightly easier to use, but all round the chest freezer is more economical.

The amount of home freezing you do on a weekly basis has to be considered, as excess use of the fast freeze can add a few pence to the weekly total. Careful and planned use of the freezer on a daily basis can help to keep the costs down slightly, by opening the door as seldom as possible and working rapidly to prevent the loss of cold air. Regular home maintenance ensures efficiency and so keeps running costs down. Having given ideas on how to cut running costs, it is unfortunately impossible to give accurate figures. These given below are intended to be a rough guide to help with freezer budgeting.

One unit of electricity costs between 1.75p – 2.25p depending on the local tariff. At the time of writing, 2p is taken as the national average.

Chest freezer

A chest freezer uses 1.25 – 1.75 units of electricity per 28 litres (1cu ft) per week. A fair example would be: 1.50 units x 10 cu ft x 2p=30p. A 10 cu ft chest freezer would cost approximately 30p per week to run.

Upright freezer

An upright freezer uses 1.50 – 2 units of electricity per 28 litres (1cu ft) per week. A fair example would be: 1.75 units x 10 cu ft x 2p=35p. A 10 cu ft upright freezer would cost approximately 35p per week to run.

Home maintenance

As with all appliances a freezer requires occasional attention, but the time involved is minimal, much less in fact than may at first be apparent. Maintenance pays three fold dividends in the long run – reduced running costs, prevention of breakdown, and slowing the rate of deterioration. There are two main areas to consider: defrosting the interior cabinet maintenance of the exterior casing.

Defrosting

A simple yet rather laborious job which must be carried out on a regular basis. Depending on location and use, an upright freezer needs to be defrosted 3–4 times per year, whilst a chest only once or twice. It is unnecessary to run stocks down to facilitate defrosting as the process should only take about an hour. Obviously it is advantageous to choose a cool day. Disconnect the freezer from the mains and stack the food in insulated bags. Put as many items as you can into the refrigerator. Having removed all accessories place one or two bowls of hot water in the bottom of the cabinet and allow to steam. Replace the water as it cools. As the ice softens gently remove with a plastic scraper. Do not use metal instruments as they can damage the interior surface. Avoid letting the ice turn to water as this makes the task rather messy.

To remove any smells wash out the interior with a solution of bicarbonate of soda. Dry thoroughly with paper towels and a soft cloth. Reconnect the freezer, and replace the washed accessories. Re-stock with food. Regular defrosting prevents a build up of ice which insulates the interior walls of the cabinet and prevents efficient running. The ice on the walls and shelves should never be more than $\frac{1}{2}$cm ($\frac{1}{4}$in) in thickness.

General hints

Some freezers have a fan attached to the motor unit to aid heat dispersal. This fan is liable to become clogged with dust and fluff if not cleaned periodically. Before attempting this ensure that the freezer is switched off at the mains. Unscrew the inlet grill and dust the fan carefully. Replace the grill and reconnect the freezer. This should be done at 6 monthly intervals.

Other freezers have a condenser grill fixed to the back of the cabinet, this should be kept free of dust at all times. Do not let objects be propped up against the unit or allow it to be used as a tea towel dryer!

A freezer sited in a damp location should be given a good coating of wax polish at regular intervals to prevent corrosion by rusting. All freezers should have breathing space to allow air circulation. 3–5cm (1–2in) is recommended all the way round. Check periodically to see that the freezer has not moved slightly as this could restrict heat dispersal. Those freezers on castors are the main offenders! For maximum efficiency check all these points regularly – the half yearly defrosting would be a convenient time.

In general freezers are very reliable and break down only occasionally. To offset this possibility some sort of maintenance contract and insurance is strongly recommended.

Quick action is necessary if the freezer does break down. A daily check of the cabinet temperature gives an accurate indication of normal running. If the temperature is too high, check:

1. Is the power supply, fuse and plug socket working properly?
2. Is the thermostat setting too low?
3. Is there dust in the motor unit?
4. Are you using the fast freeze compartment correctly?

Once you are satisfied that a minor adjustment cannot put things right, call the engineer.

Freezers tend to break down in the summer months, when the ambient temperature is high. The food will start to thaw within a matter of hours, so immediate attention is required.

Supply failure

Supply failure usually occurs in the winter and although rather inconvenient and unpleasant the freezer rarely suffers. Prior warning is usually given if supply is to be cut for more than an hour or so, so here is what to do in advance:

1. Move the freezer away from any heat which may be provided by non-electrical means.

2. Switch on to fast freeze for a couple of hours.

3. Move ice cream and cream cakes to the bottom or back of the cabinet, stacking the more dense items such as meat on the top or at the front.

4. Make sure that the freezer is well stacked and fill in the gaps with boxes and newspaper to cut down the air circulation.

5. Cover the freezer with a blanket.

6. On no account open the lid or door until the returning power has allowed the freezer to resume a normal temperature.

Under these conditions the food should be perfectly safe for 24 hours.

If the food has defrosted in extreme conditions due to breakdown or supply failure but is still chilled much of it can be salvaged by cooking and refreezing. The outside conditions will determine how long the food will remain frozen without power – the smell should determine whether the food in the freezer is still edible!

 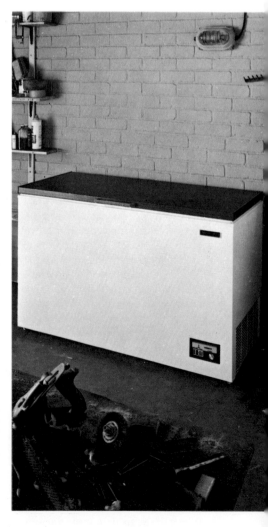

Above: An upright freezer uses less floor space than a chest freezer, but a chest freezer (right) can provide a useful work top.

Stocking the freezer

Having invested in a freezer the next task is to fill it with food. There is no easy answer to the question 'how much money can I save with a freezer?'. It could range from extremes of saving 25 per cent of the weekly budget to spending 25 per cent more. The savings are dependent on organization, careful shopping and maintaining an existing standard of living. Obviously if you allow your standard of living to rise substantially then you can not expect a cash saving into the bargain. For many people, being able to afford and enjoy better food is the initial reason for purchasing a freezer. Guide lines are perhaps unnecessary but for those intent on a cash saving here are a few suggestions.

Do not set your sights too high: a 25 per cent saving is feasible if you have a very large freezer and a lot of time to devote to it. A more realistic figure would be somewhere in the region of 10 per cent. In order to achieve this saving a certain amount of home freezing would need to be done, together with well planned shopping and good organization. Let 10 per cent be the objective. If this is exceeded then that is a bonus, but to aim for a greater saving turns the fun into a chore.

Freezing your own or buying branded products

Fruit and vegetables

The facility to store garden produce is one of the main attractions of having a freezer. For a small outlay you can have garden produce to last the whole year through. But again careful planning is essential if the money that is saved is worthy of the efforts involved.

For example if a third of the freezer were filled with runner beans, the storage costs on the beans could amount to 10p-12p per week. (for convenience, prices are given in U.K. Currency). Overstocking can prove expensive and limit the use of the freezer space for other produce. Grow and freeze a wide variety of fruit and vegetables according to the family needs. A 3–4 month supply should be maximum and store only produce which freezes well. Freezer preparation can be laborious and time consuming so bear this in mind when harvesting. Not everyone has the space, nor perhaps the inclination to grow their own produce, so the next best thing is to buy what is in season and freeze. If this is done sensibly it works well, but impulse buying can prove to be an expensive mistake – so think before you act! Take broad beans as an example:

Peak season price   10p per 500g (1lb) seems like a bargain, as the price of commercially frozen beans is about 20p per 500g (1lb). However, after preparation you are left with 400g (12oz) of pods and 100 (4oz) of beans. The true cost of the fresh beans is not 10p per 500g (1lb) but 40p per 500g (1lb). Not the bargain which initially prompted purchase.

Let us look at a product which does not incur so much wastage. The peak season price for carrots might be 5p–6p per 500g (1lb). The true price after preparation would perhaps be 8p per 500g (1lb), assuming that wastage was kept to a minimum of 1–2oz per lb. The cost of 500g (1lb) of commercially frozen carrots would be approximately 15p.

A worthwhile saving of 7p per 500g (1lb) could be achieved. It is, however, important to remember the costs of packaging materials and electricity for blanching and freezing. To allow 1p per 500g (1lb) of produce should cover these costs.

The peak season price will determine the profitability of freezing in season. It is clear how important it is to account for wastage when doing calculations.

Obviously it would be impractical to cost preparation time but it is worth bearing in mind if large quantities are involved. Money can be saved by freezing fruit and vegetables at home but these should be supplemented to a great extent by branded goods. The range of frozen branded goods available is vast and far exceeds the seasonal fresh range. Utilize the best from both. Eat some fresh and freeze the remainder in small quantities in season and use the branded goods to increase variety throughout the year. Commercially frozen vegetables and fruit, are usually superior to those frozen at home. The harvesting and preparation are done in the minimum time and the efficiency of freezing is far better than attainable in a home freezer. But the freezer owner is able to exploit the best of both worlds.

On pages 59 to 64 there is a section on gardening for freezing.

Fish

The opportunities for buying fresh fish in large quantities are limited except in certain local areas. So for the majority, commercially frozen fish is the only choice available, but as this is generally of an exceptionally high standard there should be no cause for complaint. If you are buying fresh fish do remember to account for wastage after cutting and/or filleting. There is very little wastage with some fish, but with others there is a considerable amount. The storage life is relatively short, so buy sufficient only for a 2–3 months' supply.

Meat

Meat is an expensive commodity and often comprises 30–40 per cent of the weekly budget, so to achieve a saving here must help the family income. Carcasses of meat can be attractive in price, especially in the large markets, but unless you are an experienced butcher it would be foolish to attempt jointing the meat yourself, as the wastage incurred could be substantial. Before buying check what you are paying for. Does the price include bones and fat? Is butchering included? Are they prepared to pack and freeze the meat? The true price per kilo or pound can be substantially affected by these points. On a whole or part carcass weight there is 30–40 per cent wastage. Calculate using the following formula:

$$\frac{\text{original weight} \quad \times \quad \text{cost price per kilo or pound}}{\text{net weight}} = \begin{array}{l}\text{price per kilo or pound} \\ \text{for edible meat}\end{array}$$

Example

$$\frac{45\text{kg (100lbs) gross carcass weight} \quad \times \quad 60\text{p per 500g (1lb)}}{32\text{kg (70lb) net carcass weight}} = 85.7\text{p per 500g (1lb)}$$

Therefore the carcass selling at 60p per 500g (1lb) would cost 85.7p per 500g (1lb) for edible meat.

It is an important thing to remember that if you are buying a large quantity of meat, i.e. over 45kg (100lbs) in weight, it should be frozen prior to purchase. The largest domestic freezer can only freeze 32–36kg (70–80lb) in any 24 hour period. An average sized freezer of 280–340 litres (10–12 cu ft) can freeze a maximum of 18kg (40lbs) daily, but better results would be achieved by freezing smaller quantities. Another obvious disadvantage is the amount of storage space required. 45kg (100lb) of beef would half fill a 280 litre (10 cu ft) freezer leaving little space to store other varieties of meat, let alone other produce. Of course, you do not have to buy meat in carcass weight, smaller units or individual cuts are available and for most families these are a much more practical proposition. Commercially frozen meat, despite its rather dark appearance is usually of an acceptable quality depending on the supplier. It has the advantage of being blast frozen which prevents tissue breakdown by very rapid freezing, preserving the colour, texture and flavour of the meat. The prices are competitive and there is a wide range of cuts and pack sizes to choose from. Whether buying to home freeze or buying ready frozen, quality should be the deciding factor, so shop around.

Prepared dishes

The range of frozen prepared meals increases daily – some are barely edible while others are exceptionally good. Few are cheap but some represent good value for money whilst some are exorbitant in price. This is where home freezing can be really beneficial. Depending on time available the bulk of prepared dishes both sweet and savoury should be done at home and supplemented by a range of branded convenience foods.

Almost without exception home prepared dishes taste better than branded varieties. Thus quality is improved whilst reducing the cost. Large quantities can be done at one time and stored in the freezer for 3–4 months. Many of the dishes can be made from the stocks in the freezer. Buying the raw materials in quantity has initially saved money – transferring it into prepared dishes is extending the saving.

However, it is worthwhile working out costs in advance as not all home prepared dishes show substantial saving, particularly if preparation time is taken into account. Take fish fingers as an example. To make 16 x 25g (1oz) fish fingers might cost approximately 60p, whereas a high quality branded pack would cost about 10p less. So in this instance it seems hardly worth the lengthy preparation time required when making them at home. On the other hand a home-made steak and kidney pie would cost just over half that of a bought frozen pie. Also the home-made pie would probably contain more meat in the filling and be more nutritious, and, almost certainly, more delicious! On pages 17 to 58 there are some specially prepared recipes for home prepared frozen meals. Follow these carefully and you should find they make delicious meals as well as a saving to the family budget.

Conclusion

When deciding which foods to buy and which to freeze, consider the following points.

1. Cost – Which is most economical?
2. Time – Which is the priority saving – time or money?
3. Quality and suitability – Which is of most value to the family requirements?

A selection of branded and home frozen foods is recommended. The ultimate choice is dependent on time and money available and the family needs.

Shopping

A freezer not only changes eating habits but also shopping routines. Shopping trips can be cut substantially, which must also helps the budget. Shopping for fresh produce to home freeze will depend very much on the area in which you live, but for bulk purchases farms, markets and wholesalers will probably offer the most competitive prices.

For ready frozen items, perhaps the best choice is a Freezer Food Centre, even if not conveniently located. As the shopping need only be done monthly or bi-monthly this should not cause any hardship. If transport is difficult and you do not own a car the cost of a taxi should not be ruled out. As more and more supermarket chains launch into Freezer Food Centres the competition should become keen, keeping prices down and standards high. Obviously many other retail outlets have seen the escalation of frozen food purchases and have increased their range substantially and many have mini Freezer Food Centres within the confines of their supermarkets. The choice will vary in each town, but select a specialist centre which has the widest range and most competitive prices, if this involves travelling an extra 10 miles it is generally worthwhile.

Do not however, overlook the supermarket special offers when doing the weekly shopping as these can often be very economical.

How to shop

Some people might take offence at being given advice about how to shop. Nevertheless, it is extremely important – mistakes are easily made, not only causing disappointment but often expense and wastage. If money is to be saved the following points should be remembered.

1. Less shopping will save time and money, therefore buy enough to last at least 4–6 weeks.

2. Prolonged storage will produce an inferior quality, so do not overstock on any one item.

3. Freezer space costs money, ideally stock turnover should be 4 monthly.

4. Do not experiment with too many new lines at one time and initially buy small packs rather than large packs. The bulk price may be cheaper but if the product is not to your liking you will only throw it away.

5. Buy according to your family requirements. Whether you buy for quality or price will depend on the ultimate use of the food. Good value for money is the main aim.

6. Make a shopping list but allow flexibility. If an item you want is out of stock be prepared to substitute for something else rather than making an extra trip later. Always take advantage of special offers.

7. Ask advice about unknown brands, if unsure keep to the brand leaders. Retailers own label packs are usually of an acceptable quality and a little cheaper than branded.

8. Avoid poorly packed products, but likewise do not open packs to examine the contents, ask if unsure.

9. Often large packs need repacking to accommodate in the home freezer. Ensure that the price saving compared with a smaller pack covers this inconvenience.

10. Pack frozen foods in some sort of insulated bag for transportation and aim to be home within an hour. If the food softens slightly it is perfectly safe to re-harden it. It is unnecessary to operate the fast freeze switch for this process.

Organizing the budget

The average family of 2 adults and 2 children is currently spending £14 per week on food. Transferring from a weekly to a monthly expenditure is reasonably straightforward if done in the following way. (Figures are again only hypothetical and for convenience are given in U.K. currency).

Weekly expenditure = £14

Product	Cost	Source
Meat and fish	£5	Butcher/fishmonger
Veg and fruit	£1.50	Greengrocer/supermarket
Convenience foods	£2.00	Supermarket
Groceries, eggs, bread	£4.00	Supermarket/bakers
Milk	£1.50	Milk delivery

Monthly expenditure = £56

Product	Cost Frozen	Fresh	Source
Meat and fish	£20		Freezer Food Centre
Veg and fruit	£4	£2	Freezer Food Centre and greengrocer
Convenience foods	£6	£2	Freezer Food Centre and supermarket
Groceries, eggs, bread		£16	Supermarket/bakers
Milk		£6	Milk delivery

A weekly expenditure of £14 transfers into a monthly sum of £56, obviously a five week month would be accounted for in the same way. If divided into specific categories, a sum of money can be allocated to each group of foods and this helps to prevent over-spending. The monthly expenditure breaks down:

Frozen foods £30
Fresh and groceries £26

At this stage no account has been made of possible savings with frozen food. This could be deducted at the start: i.e. £56 – 10 per cent=£50.40p but perhaps it is best to allocate the total amount as this gives more flexibility, but plan to spend within the region of £50. Obviously most of this saving will be made on the frozen foods but shopping costs will be cut and it is also possible to save by less impulse buying as the number of shopping trips has been cut. Once you are accustomed to bulk buying you may want to purchase groceries in quantity, and so add to the saving.

Working out figures in such detail may seem rather unnecessary, but if you want to see what saving you are making, it is a good idea. Often savings lose themselves in the housekeeping money, never to be revealed. So if you are looking for a true cash saving, work out a few figures – to the nearest £1 is quite sufficient.

This 10 per cent saving is also including a certain amount of home freezing, whether it be raw materials or prepared dishes, the basic ingredients still have to be purchased, whether frozen or fresh. Obviously the more profitable home freezing that can be done, the better. But a 10 per cent saving all round is quite admirable.

Working out family requirements for the months ahead requires considerable thought, and it is probably not possible to get it absolutely right. An up-to-date price list from a Freezer Food Centre is an invaluable help.

The final balance sheet could look like this:

Monthly expenditure		£56.00
Estimated savings 10 per cent		£ 5.60
Estimated expenditure		£50.40
		———
Allocation frozen food	£30 }	£26
Intended saving	£ 4 }	
Allocation fresh goods/groceries	£26 }	£24.40
Intended saving	£1.60 }	
(Transport saving 60p		
Less impulse buying 50p		———
Bulk buying groceries 50p)		£50.40p

Home freezing

For home preservation freezing is by far the simplest and most effective method. Bottling, drying, jam making are fine in their way but they change the texture and flavour of the food. Also freezing is the only effective home preservation method for produce other than fruit and vegetables.

Fast freeze

It is useful to understand the basic principles involved in freezing in order to appreciate the importance of the fast freeze compartment. Freezing has the action of turning the liquid content of the food into crystals. Fast freezing produces small crystals which form within the cell structure of the food. Slow freezing produces larger crystals which break down the interior structure, altering both the texture and flavour of the food. Switching on to fast freeze before putting in a quantity of fresh food to be frozen ensures quicker freezing and prevents a rise in the cabinet temperature which may affect the food already being stored. All freezers should reach their minimum temperature within 2 hours, so activate the fast freeze switch accordingly. All freezers are capable of freezing down 10 per cent every 24 hours of their total capacity. If the instruction book gives no indication of quantities here is a simple guide.

less in total it is not necessary to switch on to fast freeze but for other products here is a basic guide.

Meat, fish, poultry, pastries, prepared meats	2 hours per 500g (1lb)
Vegetables, fruit, dairy produce, liquids	1 hour per 500g (1lb)

Example

5 x 225g(8oz) Fillet steak	5 hours
2 x 500g (1lb) rhubarb crumble	4 hours
2 x 225g(8oz) Chocolate cakes	1 hour
3 x 500g(1lb) Brown loaves	3 hours
	13 hours

Example

2 x 500g(1lb) Shepherd's pies	4 hours
4 x 125g(4oz) Rice	2 hours
3 x 500g(1lb) Ratatouille	6 hours
	12 hours

protection against dehydration and oxidation. If however, the food is over packaged it insulates against the cold temperature and slows down the rate of freezing. Many foods can be frozen without wrapping initially. This prevents damage and allows produce to freeze separately. This method is called free-flow. However care must be taken to ensure that these food are wrapped within 12 hours otherwise slight damage could be done. There is a wide variety of packaging materials available but it should not be necessary to spend a lot of money when collecting a good stock, as many everyday polythene bags and cartons can be used.

Mix chopped herbs with a little water and freeze in cubes.

Storage capacity of a chest freezer   9kg (20lbs) per 28 litres (1 cu ft)
280 litres (10 cu ft) chest freezer
280 litres (10 cu ft) x 9kg (20lbs) per 28 litres (1cu ft)=90kg (200lbs)
        10 per cent — 90kg (200lbs) = 9kg (20lbs)

Storage capacity of an upright freezer   7kg (15lbs) per 28 litres (1 cu ft)
280 litres (10 cu ft) upright freezer
280 litres (10 cu ft) x 7kg (15lbs) per 28 litres (1 cu ft)=70kg (150lbs)
        10 per cent — 70kg (150lbs) = 7kg (15lbs)

It is unwise to leave the fast freeze device on for longer than 24 hours at a time as the motor unit can become overheated.
However, you will not always want to freeze down capacity loads. Frequently odd items require freezing and obviously they do not take so long to freeze. For quantities of 1kg (2lbs) or

Packaging for Home freezing

Correct packaging is one of the most important aspects of home freezing. All the time-consuming preparation and cost involved can result in inferior food if the packaging is not done correctly. The wrap or container is the main

Whatever method of packaging is used make sure that all the air is extracted otherwise 'frosting' will occur. It is then most important to seal the package efficiently – this is most economically achieved by twist ties and freezer tape. Labelling is also important if drastic errors are to be avoided. Stick-on labels are the most useful, but other types are available.
The following details should be recorded:–
Type of food – raw or cooked
Weight or number of portions
Date frozen or date to be used by
Special note

PACKAGING MATERIAL	USES	SEAL	RE-USABLE
Polythene Bags (120–150 gauge most suitable) Various sizes available. Relatively cheap	Meat, fish, fruit & veg. Used as a second wrapping for most items. Coloured tags are useful for identification	Twist tie Freezer tape	Yes if intact and cleaned well
Polythene and Plastic Containers Various sizes available. Must have airtight lids. The more expensive brands give better value for money in the long term	Ice-cream, soft fruits, prepared dishes, sauces	If the lid is airtight, no seal is necessary	Yes Cheap brands warp or crack if washed in very hot water
Waxed Cardboard Cartons Various types/sizes available. Tubs & boxes with snap-on lids. Cartons with moisture proof liners. Quite expensive	Liquids Sauces Soft fruits Leftovers Pâté Purée	Those with snap-on lids should not need extra sealing. Freezer tape should be used to secure others	Can be re-used until the wax begins to flake
Aluminium Foil Gauges vary. Different lengths available. Medium price	Meat, fish. Use as a protective covering before placing in a polythene bag	Effectively sealed by folding the edges closely together	If handled carefully can be re-used 2 or 3 times
Foil Containers All shapes & sizes available, some with lids, some without. Medium price (free with Chinese take away)	Plates & dishes for pies, flans etc. Deep dishes for soft fruits (not suitable for acid fruits) and prepared dishes. Use white lid for labelling	Sealed by means of lid if supplied otherwise use aluminium foil	If not used for cooking re-usable numerous times
Cotton Stockinette Sold by the metre. Expensive	Inside wrap for meat and poultry	Twist tie	Yes if washed carefully
Freezer Wraps Various types and qualities. Cling film gives the best protection although all the others are useful as an inner wrap. Inexpensive	Meat, fish. Use as a protective covering before placing in a polythene bag	Cling film is self sealing. Others require freezer tape	No
Yogurt pots and Margarine cartons	Purée Liquids Fruits Leftovers	Margarine lid usually fits well, otherwise seal with freezer tape. Cover yogurt pots with foil	Yes, if intact
Kilner jars	Liquids Soups Stock	Screw top lid	Yes
Casserole dishes	Stews and all prepared dishes	Line dish with foil, fill with cooked food. Cover with foil. When frozen, remove foil package. Place in a polythene bag.	Yes
Plastic egg cartons	Eggs Stock Small amounts of liquid	Seal the top of the carton with tape and place in a polythene bag	Twice maximum
Paper cups	Eggs Liquids Purées	Seal with aluminium foil and freezer tape	Twice maximum

Home freezing meat

Jointing a carcass is the job of a professional and it is best left to the butcher. It is wise to joint and pack the meat in the quantities required otherwise there is a tendency to use more meat and although the family eats better the savings dwindle. Careful wrapping is necessary to prevent freezer burn. This is caused when the meat is exposed to the cold temperature and it dries the meat, leaving it tough and flavourless. Double wrapping is advisable for all cuts.

Although the preparation time should not be too lengthy care must be taken to ensure that the meat is frozen ready for cooking, as most cuts can be used straight from the freezer without prior thawing.

Bacon – Joints
Bone joints if possible and roll and string.

Bacon – rashers
Pack in 225g (½lb) units inter-leaving slices if required.

Joints
Trim off excess fat. Bone, roll and string if necessary. Overwrap sharp edges to prevent damage to packaging.

Chops
Trim well removing bones where possible, wrap individually in cellophane or foil and pack into a polythene bag.

Steak
Trim off excess fat. Wrap individually and pack into polythene bag. If the steaks are large, freeze after first wrapping and pack into a polythene bag when frozen. This will preserve a good shape.

Offal
Remove excess skin and tissue and cut as required for use. Pack in 225g–450g (½–1lb) units and double wrap. Offal can be frozen free-flow if required by wrapping each piece individually.

Cubed, diced and minced meat
Trim and cut according to requirements. Wrap in 225g–450g (½–1lb) units and place several packs in a polythene bag. Label clearly as they are indistinguishable when frozen.

Poultry and game
Clean thoroughly and remove giblets. Truss the bird according to variety and close wrap twice. Alternatively joint the bird, wrap each joint individually and place into a polythene bag. Crush the carcass and use for stock.

Giblets
Double wrap and store separately. Use within 3 months.

Chicken livers
Store in plastic container. Use for pâté.

Sausages and sausage meat
Pack in 225g–450g (½–1lb) units. Double wrap.

STORAGE LIFE

Meat, poultry and game	Months
Beef and lamb	10–12
Pork and veal	4–6
Offal	3–4
Sliced bacon and other cured meats	2–3
Ham and bacon joints	3–4
Chicken and turkey	10–12
Duck and goose	4–6
Venison	10–12
Rabbit and hare	4–6
Sausages and sausage meat	2–3
Minced beef (with seasoning)	3–4
Minced beef (without seasoning)	4–6

Home freezing fish

To obtain the best results fish must be absolutely freshly caught, prepared and frozen within 24 hours if possible. If buying from the fishmongers, ask if the fish has been frozen before. Scale the fish and remove fins. Gut flat fish and herrings. Remove the head and tail from large fish but leave smaller fish whole. Freeze according to usage, a selection of cuts is useful – fillets, steaks, portions etc. Wash the fish well in slightly salted water, taking particular care with whole fish. A little lemon juice brushed over the fish helps retain colour and flavour. Double or treble wrapping is essential to preserve flavour and prevent freezer burn.

Oily fish – Haddock, halibut, mackerel, salmon, trout, turbot, whitebait. Clean and cut as required. Wrap each cut or fish separately with a double thickness of cellophane or foil and place in a polythene bag. Small fish such as whitebait should be frozen free-flow before packing into required unit packs.

White fish – Cod, plaice, sole, whiting. Clean thoroughly. Fillet or leave whole as required. Wrap separately in a double thickness of cellophane or foil and place in a polythene bag. These fish lose flavour very quickly. Thus efficient preparation and rapid freezing is essential. Always cook these fish from frozen.

Smoked fish – Eel, haddock, kippers, mackerel, salmon, sprats, trout. Prepare as for serving. Pack individually taking care to double wrap sharp edges. As many of these fish are prepared and/or eaten cold, thaw very slowly in the refrigerator.

Shellfish – Prawns, shrimps, crabs, lobsters, crayfish, oysters, mussels. Cook shrimps and prawns in boiling water until pink. Cool, remove the shell and freeze free-flow. Pack and take care to double wrap. Crabs, lobsters and crayfish should be plunged into boiling salted water for 20 minutes. After cooling remove the edible meat from shell and freeze in small units. Crabs and lobsters can be frozen whole if required. Cook oysters and mussels in the normal way before freezing. Freeze in or out of shell.

Storage life	Months
Smoked fish	4–6
White fish	6–8
Oily fish	3–4
Fish portions	3–4
Shellfish	2–3

Accessories for home freezing

Blanching basket These vary in size and quality but it is not worthwhile buying an expensive one unless it is to be used frequently. Collapsible ones are easy to store but perhaps the ridged framed blanchers are easier to use. For those who intend only to freeze small quantities of vegetables a chip basket or cotton gauze can be used instead.

Heat sealers Useful if freezing in large amounts but otherwise not worth the outlay. One or two on the market are supplied with sleeves of polythene to make bags, a useful accessory as bags can be made to the size required, but this would not be economical unless utilized regularly.

Suction pumps This is a mechanical aid to extract air from packages before freezing. They are efficient and quite cheap but a straw does the job just as well.

Stock record book A useful aid if kept up to date, as you can see at a glance the stock situation. However, many people do find this a chore.

Foods in season

To achieve the best results from home freezing only foods in prime condition should be used. This requires know-how in harvesting if the produce is from the garden, or skillful buying with a keen eye for freshness and quality.

MONTH	FRUIT	VEGETABLES	FISH	MEAT, GAME & POULTRY
JAN	Cooking apples *Cranberries* *Grapefruit* *Lemons* *Seville oranges* *Oranges* Rhubarb (early)	Brussels sprouts Cabbage Carrots Cauliflower Celery, *Chicory* Jerusalem artichokes Leeks, parsnips Turnips	Cod, haddock Mackerel Mussels Oysters Scallops, sole Sprats, turbot Whiting	Goose, turkey Hare Partridge Pheasant Pigeon Plover Snipe, wild duck Woodcock
FEB	Cooking apples Grapefruit Lemons Seville oranges *Rhubarb* (early)	Brussels sprouts Cabbage Cauliflower Celery, chicory *Leeks*, parsnips	Smoked haddock	Hare
MAR	Rhubarb (early)	*Broccoli* Brussels sprouts Cabbage Cauliflower Celery, curly-kale Parsnips	Mackerel *Oysters* *Salmon* *Scallops* *Whitebait*	Spring lamb *Duckling* Pigeon
APR	*Pineapple* Rhubarb	Broccoli Brussels sprouts Parsnips *Spinach*	Crab Mackerel *Prawns* Salmon, trout Whitebait	Spring lamb Duckling *Guinea fowl*
MAY	Pineapple Rhubarb	*Asparagus* *Broad beans* Broccoli *Carrots* Cauliflower Herbs, *peas* Spinach	*Crab*, herring *Lobster*, plaice Prawns Salmon, trout Whitebait	Spring lamb Duckling Guinea fowl
JUNE	Apricots *Cherries* *Gooseberries* Loganberries *Peaches* Raspberries Rhubarb *Strawberries*	Asparagus Broad beans *Cabbage* Carrots *Cauliflower* *Corn-on-the-cob* *French beans* *Globe artichokes* Herbs, peas *Potatoes* (new) Spinach Tomatoes	Crab, herring Lobster, plaice Prawns Salmon, shrimps Trout Whitebait	Duckling Guinea fowl

JULY			
Apricots	Asparagus	Crab, haddock	
Blackcurrants	*Aubergines*	Halibut, lobster	
Cherries, *figs*	Broad beans	Plaice, prawns	
Gooseberries	Cabbage, carrots	Red mullet	
Loganberries	Cauliflower	Salmon, shrimps	
Melons	Corn-on-the-cob	Salmon trout	
Nectarines	*Courgettes*	Sole, trout	
Peaches, plums	French beans		
Raspberries	Globe artichokes		
Redcurrants	*Herbs,* marrow		
Strawberries	Peas, *peppers*		
	Potatoes, spinach		
	Tomatoes		

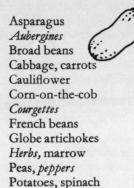

AUG			
Apples	Aubergines,	Crab, haddock,	*Grouse*
Blackberries	Beetroots (young)	Halibut, lobster	*Hare*
Damsons, figs	Cabbage	Plaice, prawns	
Melons	Cauliflower	Salmon, sole	
Peaches	Corn-on-the-cob	Trout, turbot	
Pears, plums	French beans		
	Globe artichokes		
	Peas, peppers		
	Runner beans		
	Spinach, *tomatoes*		

SEPT			
Apples	Aubergines	Crab, haddock	*Goose*
Blackberries	Brussels sprouts	Halibut, herring	Turkey
Damsons, grapes	Cabbage, cauliflower	Lobster, oysters	Grouse, hare
Peaches, pears	Celery	Plaice, prawns	*Partridge*
Plums	Corn-on-the-cob	Sole, turbot	*Rabbit, snipe*
	Courgettes, leeks		*Venison*
	Mushrooms, *onions*		*Wild duck*
	Parsnips, peppers		*Woodcock*
	Pimentos, runner beans		
	Spinach, swedes		
	Tomatoes		

OCT			
Apples	*Brussels sprouts*	Cod, haddock	Beef, turkey
Blackberries	Cabbage, *celery*	Herring	Grouse, hare
Damsons, *grapes*	Leeks, parsnips	Mackerel	Partridge
Nuts, pears	Spinach, *swedes*	Oysters	*Pheasant*
Pomegranates	*Turnips*	Plaice	Snipe
Pumpkins, *quince*		Scallops, sole	Venison
		Sprats, turbot	Wild duck

NOV			
Apples	Brussels sprouts	Cod, haddock	Goose
Cranberries	Cabbage, celery	Herring	Turkey
Grapes, nuts	Jerusalem artichokes	Mackerel, oysters	Hare
Pears, pomegranates	Leeks, parsnips	Plaice, scallops	Partridge
Tangerines	Red cabbage, swedes	Sole, sprats	Pheasant
	Turnips	Turbot, whiting	Snipe, wild duck

DEC			
Apples, cranberries	Brussels sprouts	Cod, haddock	Goose, turkey
Grapes, nuts	Cabbage, celery	Herring, mackerel	Hare, partridge
Pomegranates	Celeriac, Jerusalem	Oysters, plaice	Pheasant
Tangerines	artichokes, leeks	Scallops, sole	Snipe
	Parsnips, swedes	Sprats, turbot	Wild duck
	Turnips	Whiting	

Recommended product in each month is in italics.

11

Home freezing fruit

As with vegetables choose only fruit of a high quality and preferably slightly under-ripe. Damaged or over-ripe fruit should be puréed or liquidized to make fruit juices. When preparing fruit avoid using galvanized iron, copper or brass as the utensils may discolour or taint the produce. There are several ways of freezing fruit and the choice will depend on the texture of the fruit and its intended use after freezing.

Freezing free-flow
This is the ideal method for freezing fruit in prime condition as there are no additives which may restrict use. Clean the fruit thoroughly but avoid washing if possible. Spread the fruit evenly on lined baking sheets or trays and freeze uncovered. Repack in suitable containers. Specks of dirt and small stalks will 'freeze off' leaving the fruit clean.

Dry sugar packs
Having cleaned the fruit lay evenly on sheets of greaseproof paper. Sprinkle liberally with sugar allowing 113g per ¼kg (4oz per lb) of fruit. Leave for several minutes until the juices begin to flow from the fruit then roll the fruit gently in the sugar syrup until well coated. Pack in rigid containers allowing 1cm(½in) headspace for expansion.

Sugar syrup
Prepare the fruit and divide into 500g (1lb) units. Cover each pound of fruit with 300ml (½ pint) of sugar syrup. Place a double layer of cellophane over the top and seal tightly leaving 1cm (½ inch) headspace. Sugar syrup: add 350g (12oz) sugar to 600ml (1 pint) boiling water, simmer for several minutes. Allow to cool before use.

FRUIT	PREPARATIONS	METHOD OF FREEZING	STORAGE LIFE
Apples	Peel, core and slice into cold salted water. Steam blanch for ½–1 minute.	Free-flow	10 months
Apricots	Choose firm, ripe well-coloured fruit. Cut in half and remove stone.	Sugar syrup	12 months
Blackberries	Large ripe fruit are preferable.	Free-flow	12 months
Blackcurrants Redcurrants Blueberries	A ½ minute blanch helps to prevent skins toughening, but is not necessary. If freezing unblanched, top and tail when frozen.	Free-flow	12 months
Cherries	Choose acid red varieties for cooking. Black varieties for desserts. Remove stone.	Sugar syrup	12 months
Citrus fruits	Ripe fruit should be used for juice and grated peel. Slices can be frozen individually for drinks or decoration. Seville oranges can be frozen whole for future marmalade making.	Free-flow	12 months
Cranberries	Clean and stalk.	Dry sugar	12 months
Gooseberries	Stew before freezing for best results although plain or syrup packs can be used. Skins tend to go a little tougn during freezing.	Free-flow	12 months
Greengages, Damsons and Plums	Halve and stone.	Dry sugar	12 months
Loganberries	Choose underipe fruit.	Free-flow	12 months
Melon	Do not attempt to freeze in the skin. Ball, cube or slice depending on intended use.	Sugar syrup	12 months
Peaches	Choose firm ripe fruit. Blanch ½ minute. Remove the skin and stone.	Sugar syrup	8 months
Pears	Peel and halve and keep submerged in salted water, poach in syrup for 2 minutes. This helps to retain the colour.	Sugar syrup	12 months
Pineapple	Peel the fruit and cut into slices or chunks.	Dry sugar	12 months
Raspberries	Choose firm raspberries. Clean carefully but avoid washing.	Free-flow	12 months
Rhubarb	Choose young tender stalks. Cut in 3cm (1 inch) cubes.	Dry sugar	12 months
Strawberries	Best frozen puréed as they go rather soft during freezing.		12 months

Home freezing vegetables

Freeze vegetables within 24 hours of being picked, and choose only young vegetables. Clean the vegetables carefully discarding any which are inferior and sort into uniform portions.

Blanching

Blanching retards enzyme action and ensures a top quality frozen vegetable. Bring 3½ litres (6 pints) of water to the boil in a large pan. Place ½kg (1 lb) of vegetables into a blanching basket or muslin bag and plunge into the boiling water. Return to boiling point and time the blanching process carefully according to the chart below. Under-blanching results in colour change and loss of nutrients whilst over-blanching changes texture and flavour. After blanching the vegetables must be cooled very quickly. This is best achieved by placing them in a bowl of ice-chilled water for several minutes. When cool drain well and lay on kitchen paper. Vegetables can be frozen free-flow or in family unit blocks. The amount of freezing being done will determine the choice as freezing free-flow takes up a lot of freezer space. However, it does give better results with some vegetables.

Place one layer of vegetables on a baking sheet or similar tray and place in the freezer. When the vegetables are frozen repack into polythene bags or boxes.

Packing into family units is simpler and less time consuming. Pack into 110g (¼ lb), 225g (½ lb) or 450g (1 lb) units depending on requirements and label accordingly. As all vegetables are cooked straight from the freezer this method should cause no problems as long as the unit sizes are correct. Damaged or over-ripe vegetables can be frozen in puréed form and used as a basis for stocks and soups.

VEGETABLE	PREPARATIONS	BLANCHING TIME (in minutes)	METHOD OF FREEZING & PACKING	STORAGE LIFE
Asparagus	Select stalks which are young and tender. Grade by thickness for blanching.	Thin stalks – 2 Thick stalks – 4	Freeze free-flow Pack in boxes.	9 months
Artichokes Globe	Remove the 'heart' and discard all outer leaves. Adding lemon juice to the blanching water helps to retain a good colour.	6	Freeze free-flow Pack in boxes.	12 months
Artichokes Jerusalem	Peel and cut into slices, simmer gently in chicken stock and purée.		Freeze in units. Pack in boxes.	3 months
Beans – Broad	Pod and grade using only young tender beans.	3	Freeze in units. Pack in polythene bags.	12 months
Beans – French	Choose beans which snap cleanly and are not stringy. Trim ends – leave whole.	2	Freeze in units. Pack in polythene bags.	12 months
Beans – Runner	String and trim, slice coarsely or cut.	2	Freeze in units. Pack in polythene bags.	12 months
Beetroot	Use young beetroot not more than 5–8cm (2–3 in) in diameter. Cook thoroughly for 10–15 minutes according to size. Cool, slice cube or leave whole as preferred.		Freeze free-flow Pack in boxes.	6 months
Broccoli	Choose compact heads. Divide sprigs so that they are 3–5cm (1–2 in) wide, 8cm (3 in) long. Remove woody stalks.	3	Freeze free-flow. Pack in boxes.	12 months
Brussels Sprouts	Select firm, tight sprouts not more than 3cm (1 in) in diameter. Trim outer leaves and make a cut in the stem.	3	Freeze in units. Pack in polythene bags.	12 months
Cabbage White & Red	Cut into wedges or shred Frozen cabbage is not suitable for use as a salad vegetable.	Wedges – 2 Shredded – 1	Freeze in units. Pack in polythene bags.	6 months
Carrots	For small whole carrots, remove tops. After blanching cool under running water when skins may be rubbed off at the same time.	Whole – 4 Sliced – 2	Freeze in units. Pack in polythene bags.	12 months

VEGETABLE	PREPARATIONS	BLANCHING TIME (in minutes)	METHOD OF FREEZING & PACKING	STORAGE LIFE
Cauliflower	Break into florets of even size 4–5cm (1½–2 in) diameter. Adding lemon juice to the blanching helps retain good colour.	3	Freeze in units. Pack in polythene bags.	9 months
Celery	Choose crisp, tender celery, remove outer stalks and cut into 3cm (1 in) pieces. Celery hearts should be trimmed to 8–10cm (3–4 in) removing all coarse outer stalks. Frozen celery is not suitable for use as a salad vegetable.	Hearts – 6–8 Stalks – 3	Freeze in units. Pack in polythene bags.	9 months
Corn-on-the-cob	Choose tender, but not overripe corn. Remove husk and silk. Ensure the centres are completely cool before packing. For corn kernels cut the kernels from the cob after blanching.	4–8 according to size	Freeze free-flow. Pack in polythene bags.	12 months
Courgettes	Select young, tender courgettes. Leave whole or cut in 3cm (1 in) slices.	Whole – 2 Sliced – 1	Freeze in units. Pack in polythene bags.	12 months
Marrow	Peel and seed the marrow. Cook until soft and mash.		Freeze in units. Pack in boxes.	12 months
Mushrooms	Choose only small white mushrooms. Cook gently in a little butter for 5 minutes. Drain well.		Freeze free-flow. Pack in polythene bags.	6 months
Onions	Peel, slice or leave whole. Double wrap to ensure smell does not penetrate into freezer.	2	Freeze in units. Pack in polythene bags.	6 months
Parsnips, Turnips and Swede	Freeze only young, tender vegetables. Prepare in the usual way and dice, slice or leave whole if small.	Whole – 4 Diced – 2	Freeze in units. Pack in polythene bags.	12 months
Peas	Young, tender peas only. Pod and grade. Discard any that are tough or discoloured.	1	Freeze free-flow. Pack in polythene bags.	12 months
Peppers	Remove seeds and pith. Leave whole, quarter or dice – a selection of various types is useful.	3	Freeze in polythene bags	12 months
Potatoes – new	Only small, tender potatoes are suitable. Scrape and cook almost completely in the normal way.		Freeze free-flow. Pack in polythene bags.	9 months
Potatoes – old	Cook until tender, mash and cream. Freeze as croquettes or duchess potatoes.		Freeze free-flow. Pack in boxes.	6 months
Potatoes – chips	Prepare potatoes in the usual way and deep-fat fry until just turning to a pale brown colour. Drain on absorbent paper. Cool.		Freeze free-flow. Pack in polythene bags.	6 months
Spinach	Pick over leaves carefully – remove discoloured parts and woody stalks. Blanch in small quantities and shake frequently to ensure a thorough penetration.	2	Freeze in units. Pack in polythene bags.	12 months
Tomatoes	Freeze whole or in halves. Prepare as purée or juice. Blanching is not necessary.		Freeze free-flow. Pack in polythene bags.	6 months

Cooking frozen foods

Most recipes or home-made concoctions will freeze, some more successful than others, although inevitably there is a certain amount of trial and error. Do not be afraid to experiment with small portions, perhaps the odd amendment may be necessary, but freezing rarely affects the dish. Always freeze down in family or individual portions for easy use, it relieves the irritation of trying to separate frozen food and it saves the unnecessary job of re-freezing.

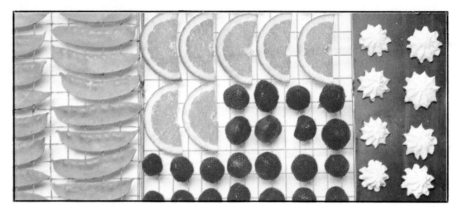

Hints for home preparation

1. Use seasonings sparingly, excess amounts alter the flavour quite noticeably, garlic and curry are particularly prone to flavour change. Add extra herbs, spices and seasonings on re-heating if required.
2. Wine or other alcohol if used in small quantities is not affected by the freezing process. More can be added on re-heating if necesasry.
3. Pre-cooked dishes to be served hot will require re-heating. So it is wise to undercook by approximately 30 minutes.
4. Pastry dishes should be cooked straight from the freezer. To allow for this it may be necessary to pre-cook the filling.
5. Frozen pastry can be thawed and refrozen without cooking when making pies and other dishes.
6. To prevent the base pastry of a pie going soggy, line the dish with pastry and freeze. Remove from the freezer, complete the pie with filling and crust and return to the freezer.
7. To economize on freezer accessories, line normal cookware with foil before preparation. Once frozen remove the foil package from the dish and seal in a polythene bag. Re-heat by placing in the original dish.
8. If freezing down large quantities of stew, pour into a roasting tin and freeze free-flow for a couple of hours. Before it is completely frozen cut into brick shapes and wrap in foil. This is economical on freezer space as all the packages are the same shape.
9. Fruit juices, stock, sauces and soups

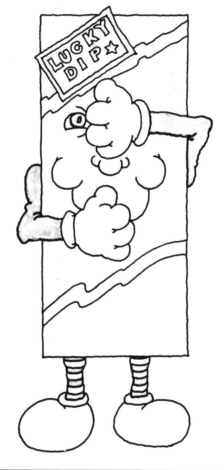

should be frozen in concentrated portions by reducing the water content. Ice cube trays are a handy item, as portions can be frozen individually then stored in polythene bags.

10. If you freeze liquids in a container leave 1cm ($\frac{1}{2}$ inch) headspace for expansion.
11. Do not use too much thickening agent in any dish, this is better done at the re-heating stage.
12. Cakes and biscuits should be frozen baked but undecorated. Freeze them uncovered to prevent damage then wrap carefully in foil or polythene.
13. Bread and dough products are particularly susceptible to dehydration and should be carefully double wrapped. Bread dough freezes particularly well and is economical on freezer space.
14. Sandwiches should be made with fresh, decrusted bread. Avoid using salad vegetables, hard boiled eggs and mayonnaise. Sliced meats, cheese and spreads are the most successful.
15. Always label clearly, once frozen it is difficult to distinguish one dish from another.
16. Avoid freezing in large units. For catering purposes or for entertaining freeze in 4–6 portions only. When thawing, re-heating and serving, smaller sizes are more manageable.
17. The storage life of many pre-cooked dishes is limited, so do not overstock the freezer with any one particular item.
18. Always refrigerate dishes before placing in the freezer.
19. Avoid using double cream as it has a tendency to curdle.

Storage life for prepared dishes	Months
Ready-prepared meals – highly seasoned	2–3
Ready-prepared meals – average seasoning	4–6
Boil-in-the-bag meals	4–6
Cakes	4–6
Bread – all kinds	2–3
Sandwiches	2–3
Bread dough	2–3
Other yeast products and pastries	3–4

Meat, poultry and game

Roasting joints

Only joints under 2½kg (5lbs) in weight should be cooked from frozen, otherwise the cooking time becomes very lengthy. A meat thermometer is a useful aid as it helps to establish when the joint is cooked to requirement. Cook bags are becoming increasingly popular and provide a successful way for this method of cooking, as they are self basting and require no extra fat. Open roasting, or foil, can be substituted but frequent basting is required.

1. Pre-heat oven to:
   180°C (350°F) Mark 4 1½kg (3lbs) and under
   170°C (325°F) Mark 3 1½–2½kg (3–5lbs)
2. Put the joint in a cook bag and seal with a twist tie. Place in a shallow roasting tin and position centrally in the oven.
3. Calculate the approximate cooking time according to preference:

Minutes per 450g (1lb)

	Rare	Medium	Well done
Beef	45	50	60
Lamb	45	50	60
Pork	50	60	75

4. Half an hour before the end of the estimated cooking time take a reading with thermometer and adjust the cooking time accordingly.

If a crisp exterior is required, slit the bag at this point.
5. When cooked, cut open the bag and remove the joint. Use the excess meat juices for gravy or sauce.

Steaks and chops

Grilling and frying both give satisfactory results. It is difficult to give accurate cooking times as thickness and size have an obvious bearing. A general guide would be just less than twice that for thawed meat. Cook under a low heat and baste frequently.

Slow cooking joints

Brisket, pot roast, rolled breast of lamb and other slow cooking joints should be cooked from frozen but on a reduced temperature and for an extended cooking time. The cooking time should be approximately double that for roasting joints:

Minutes per 450g (1lb)

	Rare	Medium	Well done
Beef	90	100	120
Lamb	90	100	120

If roasting, use a cook bag and follow the method above. With pot roasting or braising, simmer very slowly adding vegetables and other ingredients one hour before the end of cooking time.

Other cuts

Mince, braising and stewing meats are best simmered in stock until defrosted. In this way none of the juices are lost. The meat can then be used as you require.

Poultry and game

Whole carcasses must be thawed before cooking otherwise it is difficult to establish when the bird is thoroughly cooked. Joints or portions can be cooked from frozen.

Fish

Fish can be successfully cooked from frozen by any traditional method, grilling, frying, poaching, baking or steaming and in fact benefits from it. The delicate flavour of fish can be lost in the thawing process if carelessly carried out. However, care must be taken not to over-cook, this makes the flesh dry and flaky. Add a third to the normal cooking time on a reduced heat. Baste frequently, particularly when grilling.

Vegetables and fruit

Frozen vegetables require a reduced cooking time rather than an extended one. There are two reasons. Firstly the vegetables are frozen in prime condition when young and tender, so from the beginning the minimum cooking time is required. Secondly, the blanching process partially cooks the vegetable, necessitating the cooking time to be reduced. Over-cooking reduces the nutritive value and often renders the food soggy and flavourless. For the best results they should be added to a small amount of salted boiling water and cooked for a minimum number of minutes.

Examples:

Asparagus	3–5 minutes
Carrots	5–7 minutes
Broad Beans	5–7 minutes
Broccoli	5–7 minutes
Brussels Sprouts	3–5 minutes
Cauliflower	5–7 minutes
Sliced Beans	2–4 minutes
Peas	2–4 minutes
Mixed Vegetables	5–7 minutes
Spinach	3–5 minutes

Many vegetables can be successfully cooked in the oven. This is economical on fuel especially if the oven is in use. Place the vegetables in a shallow dish with 28–55g (1–2oz) of butter or margarine. Cover closely with foil. Cooking time will vary according to the vegetable and the oven temperature. Fruits that are used frequently in pies and other cooked desserts, should be used in their frozen state, and cooked within the dish. For stewing use only a small amount of water. The exact quantity will depend on the fruit itself. If the fruit is simmered very gently, no water is required.

Recipes

There is nothing magical about recipes for freezing – do not think that the only recipes you can use are those which come from a Freezer Book. Often recipes for freezing have to be adapted only in minor ways, for example, adding the cream before serving rather than before freezing as in Iced Carrot Soup or, reducing the cooking time in other recipes to allow for the extra cooking which is inevitable in the heating-up process after freezing. The instructions given in these recipes should also give you a guide to adapting any traditional recipes which you may wish to freeze.

The list of ingredients includes both fresh and frozen items – but it may be economical for you to use foods in another form, for example, where

300 ml (½ pint) stock is required, you may use cubes or powdered brands, but preferably as a freezer owner, home prepared stock cubes (frozen in concentrate units) should be available from the freezer. Lemon slices and chopped parsley for garnish should be stored in the freezer when cheap and used throughout the year rather than paying expensive out-of-season prices.

As a freezer owner, learn to be adaptable not only when converting recipes for freezer use, but also when using freezer recipes. Foods taken from the freezer and used in cooked dishes can always be refrozen. One useful point to remember – pastry can be thawed and refrozen without cooking: it in no way affects the product.

In almost all recipes, thawing times are

given and it is recommended that everything should be thawed in the refrigerator – slow thawing results in better eating. However, it must be remembered that refrigerator temperatures vary considerably and if your refrigerator reading is 4°C (40°F), or below, longer thawing times may be necessary. The times quoted in the recipe section are for a refrigerator reading of about 7°C (45°F).

There is no hard and fast rule as to whether prepared dishes should be thawed before reheating or cooked from the freezer. Each method has its advantages – the thawed product takes less time to cook, whereas the frozen product can be used straight from the freezer and so eliminating the laborious job of planning 24 hours ahead.

Party dishes

Smoked Mackerel Pâté   Ⓛ Ⓛ

12 SERVINGS	Metric/UK/	US
Large smoked mackerel, thawed	4/4	4
Butter	225g/8oz	1 cup
Horseradish sauce	6 tablespoons	6 tbsp
Lemons	4/4	4
Slices of white bread	8/8	8
Salt and pepper		

Carefully skin and remove the bones from the mackerel. Melt the butter, squeeze the lemons.

Remove the crust from the bread and soak the bread in water for a few minutes. Take out and squeeze dry.

Mix together the damp bread, melted butter, horseradish sauce and the lemon juice with a little salt and a generous amount of freshly ground pepper.

Break up the mackerel flesh with a fork, and add it to the bread mixture. Blend thoroughly and divide the mixture into 2 portions.

To freeze: Spoon each portion into a container. Seal, label and freeze.

To serve: Thaw in the refrigerator for 12 hours. Transfer the pâté to a serving dish and garnish with parsley sprigs and lemon slices and serve with hot toast.

Above: Smoked Mackerel Pâté is simple to prepare.
Right: Artichokes stuffed with Pork and Almonds.

Potted Chicken   Ⓛ Ⓛ

About 1¼kg [3lb]	Metric/UK/	US
Roasting chicken, thawed	1x1.75kg [approx]	
	1x4lb	1x4lb
Salt and pepper		
Butter	675g/1½lb	3 cups
Garlic clove, crushed	1/1	1
Juice of half a lemon		
Mace	1 teaspoon	1 tsp
Nutmeg	1 teaspoon	1 tsp
Salt	2 teaspoons	2 tsp
Cayenne pepper	½ teaspoon	½ tsp

Heat the oven to 190°C (Gas Mark 5, 375°F).

Season the chicken inside and out with plenty of salt and pepper. Rub the skin with 113g (4oz) [½ cup] of butter. Make a few incisions in the flesh and insert the garlic. Wrap the chicken loosely in aluminium foil and roast until well cooked (1½ hours or more).

When the chicken is cool, remove the skin and bones and finely mince the meat. Add ½kg (1lb) [2 cups] of butter, the lemon juice and remaining seasonings and beat together until a smooth paste is obtained. Press the mixture into a freezer-tested mould or moulds.

Clarify the remaining 113g (4oz) [½ cup] of butter and pour over the potted chicken to seal.

To freeze: Seal, label and freeze.

To serve: Thaw in the refrigerator for 12-24 hours, depending on the size of the mould used. When thawed turn potted chicken out on to a serving dish.

Artichokes Stuffed with Pork and Almonds

4 SERVINGS	Metric/UK/	US
Large artichokes	4/4	4
1 lemon quartered		
Lemon juice	50ml/2fl oz	¼ cup
Enough boiling water to cover the artichokes		
Salt	1 tablespoon	1 tbsp
STUFFING		
Vegetable fat	50g/2oz	¼ cup
Minced [ground] pork, thawed	225g/½lb	½lb
Frozen onion, chopped	125g/4oz	4oz
Fresh breadcrumbs	50g/2oz	1 cup
Chopped parsley	2 tablespoons	2 tbsp
Salt	½ teaspoon	½ tsp
Freshly ground black pepper		
Celery salt	½ teaspoon	½ tsp
Blanched almonds, finely chopped	50g/2oz	½ cup
Egg, lightly beaten	1/1	1
Vegetable oil	1 tablespoon	1 tbsp

Wash and prepare the artichokes for boiling. Squeeze lemon juice over the cut areas to prevent them discolouring. Using a sharp knife, cut off the top third of each artichoke. Pull open the centre leaves carefully and pull out the yellow and purple leaves from the centres. Using a teaspoon scrape and pull off all the fuzzy chokes to expose the heart. Squeeze a little lemon juice into the hollows. Push the leaves back together again.

Stand the artichokes in a large saucepan. If they do not fit snugly into the saucepan, tie a piece of string around each one so they will keep their shape while boiling.

Pour the boiling water and the remaining lemon juice over the artichokes so that they are completely covered. Add the salt. Cover the saucepan and simmer the artichokes, over medium heat, for 25 minutes, or until the bases are tender when pierced with a sharp knife. When the artichokes are cooked, remove them from the water with a slotted spoon and turn them upside down in a colander to drain.

In a large, heavy frying pan, melt the fat, Add the pork and the onions and sauté them until they are lightly browned. Remove the frying pan from the heat and add the breadcrumbs, parsley, salt, 4 grindings of pepper, celery salt, almonds and beaten egg.

Stir the mixture well.

Place the artichokes in a baking dish and fill the centres with the stuffing.

To freeze: Cool completely. Pack the artichokes into a large rigid container. Seal, label and freeze.

To serve: Preheat the oven to 180°C (Gas Mark 4, 350°F). Transfer the frozen artichokes to a baking dish.

Pour a little water around the artichokes. Brush the artichokes generously with oil. Cover the dish with aluminium foil and bake on the centre shelf of the oven for 50-60 minutes until the artichokes are tender.

Serve hot. Ⓛ Ⓛ

Chicken Kiev

Ⓛ Ⓛ

4 SERVINGS	Metric/UK/	US
Butter	125g/4oz	½ cup
Chopped fresh parsley	1 tablespoon	1 tbsp
Chopped fresh chives	1 tablespoon	1 tbsp
Garlic clove, crushed	1/1	1
Salt	½ teaspoon	½ tsp
Freshly ground black pepper	½ teaspoon	½ tsp
Chicken breast halves, thawed, skinned and boned	8/8	8
Flour	50g/2oz	½ cup
Eggs, lightly beaten	2/2	2
Fine dry white breadcrumbs	175g/6oz	2 cups
Sufficient vegetable oil for deep-frying		

In a medium-sized mixing bowl, cream the butter with a wooden spoon. When it is soft, beat in the parsley, chives, garlic, salt and pepper. Divide the butter mixture into 8 pieces (one for each breast half) and shape them into small, oval pieces. Place the pieces of butter mixture in the refrigerator.

Place one chicken breast half between 2 sheets of greaseproof or waxed paper on a chopping board and pound it thin with a mallet or similar heavy object. Flatten the remaining chicken breast halves in the same way.

Remove the greaseproof or waxed paper and wrap the chicken breast halves around the butter mixture envelope-fashion so that each piece is tubular in shape with the butter sealed in.

Put the flour, beaten eggs and breadcrumbs into 3 separate shallow bowls and set them side by side on the kitchen table. Dip the chicken breasts, one by one, first into the flour, then into the egg (make sure that each piece is thoroughly coated with the egg mixture) and, finally, into the breadcrumbs. Each piece should have a fairly thick layer of breadcrumbs.

To freeze: Freeze free-flow for 6-8 hours. Close wrap individually in foil and pack in a rigid container. A polythene [plastic] bag can be used instead of a rigid container as a second wrap but care must be taken not to damage the chicken breasts during storage as the breadcrumbs may fall off. Seal and label.

To serve: Preheat the oven to very cool 130°C (Gas Mark ½ 250°F).

In a large pan suitable for deep-frying, heat the oil until it reaches 185°C (360°F) on a fat thermometer, or until a small piece of dry bread dropped into the hot oil turns golden in 50 seconds.

Use a frying basket if you have one; this makes it easier to remove the chicken breasts the moment they are ready. Fry the breasts two at a time, for about 10-12 minutes each, or until they are golden brown in colour. As each batch is cooked, place them on a baking sheet lined with kitchen paper towels and then put them in the oven to keep warm.

Above left: For Chicken Kiev, wrap the flattened chicken breasts around the butter mixture, envelope-fashion.
Above right: Dip the stuffed breasts first into the flour then in the beaten egg, then in breadcrumbs.
Left: After deep-frying, drain on kitchen paper.
Right: Allspice Veal Roll is attractive and easy to prepare.

Allspice Veal Roll

Ⓛ Ⓛ

4 SERVINGS	Metric/UK/	US
Breast of veal, thawed, boned and trimmed of excess fat	900g/2lb	2lb
White breadcrumbs	50g/2oz	1 cup
Raisins or sultanas	1 tablespoon	1 tbsp
Grated rind of 1 orange		
Finely chopped parsley	1 tablespoon	1 tbsp
Dried sage	¼ teaspoon	¼ tsp
Dried thyme	¼ teaspoon	¼ tsp
Frozen onion, finely chopped	25g/1oz	1oz
Salt	¼ teaspoon	¼ tsp
Freshly ground black pepper		
Butter, cut into pieces	40g/1½oz	3 tbsp
Ground allspice	1 tablespoon	1 tbsp
Softened butter	25g/1oz	2 tbsp
Butter, melted	50g/2oz	2 tbsp
Orange juice	3 tablespoons	3 tbsp

Preheat oven to moderate 180°C (Gas Mark 4, 350°F).

Mix together the breadcrumbs, raisins, or sultanas, orange rind, parsley, sage, thyme and the onion.

Put the veal flat on your work surface fat side down. Spread the breadcrumb mixture evenly on the meat. Sprinkle with salt and 4 grindings of pepper. Dot with small pieces of butter. Roll the meat up tightly and tie round with string at 3cm (1 inch) intervals.

Rub the outer surface of the veal roll with the softened butter creamed with the ground allspice. Put in a baking dish with melted butter. Pour the orange juice over the meat.

Bake in the centre of the oven, basting occasionally, adding more orange juice if the liquid in the pan reduces too much. Allow 25 minutes to the pound.

To freeze: Cool. Close wrap the roll in foil and place in a polythene [plastic] bag. Seal, label and freeze.

To serve: Preheat the oven to 180°C (Gas Mark 4, 350°F). Cook the frozen roll in the oven for 30-40 minutes. Transfer the veal roll to a heated serving plate, remove the string and serve garnished with thin orange slices.

Boeuf en Croûte   Ⓛ Ⓛ

12 SERVINGS	Metric/UK/	US
Fresh fillet of beef	1x2kg [approx]	
	1x4½lb	1x4½lb
Freshly ground pepper		
Butter	75g/3oz	⅜ cup
Frozen button mushrooms	225g/8oz	8oz
Chopped parsley	4 tablespoons	4 tbsp
Salt	½ teaspoon	½ tsp
Good quality liver pâté, thawed	175g/6oz	6oz
Puff pastry, thawed	350g/12oz	3 cups
Egg, beaten	1/1	1

Heat oven to 200°C (Gas Mark 6, 400°F).

Trim off all the excess fat and sinew from the meat. Roll into a neat bolster and tie with fine string at intervals to secure the shape. Dust with pepper.

Heat the butter in a frying-pan and brown the meat all over.

Transfer the beef to a roasting tin and roast in the oven for 10 minutes.

Take out and leave to cool. Remove the string.

Slice the mushrooms, and sauté in the butter left from the meat, mix with the parsley and a little salt and leave to cool.

Roll out the pastry to a rectangle about 3mm (⅛ inch) thick, and large enough to easily cover the meat.

Spread the pâté and the mushrooms over the top and sides of the fillet, and place it, pâté side down, in the centre of the pastry. Then spread pâté on the remaining side.

Beat the egg and brush along the edges of the pastry, and fold the pastry over the meat, pressing the two sides firmly together. Brush the pastry ends with egg and fold up, cutting away any surplus pastry. Use this for making pastry leaves. Decorate centre of pastry case without the join.

To freeze: Freeze free-flow for 6-8 hours to prevent crushing the pastry decoration. Close wrap in foil and place in a rigid container. A polythene [plastic] bag can be used as a second wrap but care must be taken during storage not to damage the pastry case. Seal and label.

To serve: Preheat the oven to 180°C (Gas Mark 4, 350°F).

Place the Boeuf en Croûte on a baking sheet, pastry join down, brush with egg.

Bake in the centre of the oven for 30-40 minutes until the pastry is golden brown.

Serve hot or cold.

Homard Provençale   Ⓛ

4 SERVINGS	Metric/UK/	US
Cooked lobsters, shells split, claws cracked and grey sac removed, thawed	2x900g/2x2lb	2x2lb
Butter	50g/2oz	¼ cup
Olive oil	2 tablespoons	2 tbsp
Frozen onion, finely chopped	125g/4oz	4oz
Garlic clove, crushed	1/1	1
Tomatoes, thawed, peeled and chopped	6/6	6
Tomato purée	50g/2oz	¼ cup
Dried thyme	1 teaspoon	1 tsp

	Metric/UK	US
Dried basil	½ teaspoon	½ tsp
Salt	½ teaspoon	½ tsp
Black pepper	¼ teaspoon	¼ tsp
Saffron	⅛ teaspoon	⅛ tsp

Remove the lobster meat from the shells and claws and cut it into 5cm (2 inch) pieces.

In a large frying pan, melt the butter with the oil over moderate heat. When the foam subsides, add the frozen onion and garlic and fry them for 4 minutes.

Add the tomatoes, tomato purée, thyme, basil, salt, pepper and saffron.

Cover the pan, reduce the heat to low and simmer for 20 minutes. Stir in the lobster pieces.

To freeze: Cool. Place the provençale in a rigid container. Seal, label and freeze.

To serve: Thaw over a gentle heat stirring frequently. Cook for a further 2-3 minutes.

Remove the pan from the heat and turn the mixture into a warmed serving dish. Serve on a bed of rice.

Left: Homard Provençale and (right) Boned and Roast Duck with Oranges will impress your dinner party guests.

Boned and Roast Stuffed Duck with Oranges Ⓛ Ⓛ

8 SERVINGS	Metric/UK/	US
Duck, thawed	2½kg/5lb	5lb
Calf or lamb liver, thawed	450g/1lb	1lb
Pork sausagemeat, thawed	450g/1lb	1lb
Chopped parsley	1 tablespoon	1 tbsp
Clove garlic, crushed	1/1	1
Brandy [optional]	1 tablespoon	1 tbsp
Salt and pepper		
Medium-sized oranges	3/3	3

Place the duck, breast side down, on a wooden board. Using a very sharp, and fairly small knife, cut through the back skin down to the back bone, and then carefully work the flesh away from the carcass, pressing the knife against the carcass and taking all the meat away from the bone with the skin.

Remove the bones from the legs and wings by scraping the flesh away, but leave the drumstick bones in place. Mince [grind] the calf or lamb liver and mix with the sausagemeat, parsley, garlic and brandy if used. Season well with salt and pepper. Peel the oranges, removing all the white pith, then cut each orange in half lengthways. Open out the duck and remove any excess fat.

Spread half the liver mixture down the centre of the duck, then lay the orange halves along the stuffing with their cut sides uppermost. Spread the remaining stuffing over the oranges. Fold the ends of the duck in over the stuffing, then fold the sides into the centre to form a parcel. Sew the edges together with fine string or coarse thread.

To freeze: Close wrap the duck in foil and place in a polythene [plastic] bag. Seal, label and freeze.

To serve: Thaw in the refrigerator for 24 hours. Preheat the oven to 200°C (Gas Mark 6, 400°F).

Prick the skin of the duck all over with a fork. Roast uncovered for 20 minutes, then lower the temperature to 180°C (Gas Mark 4, 350°F) and roast for a further 1 hour 40 minutes. Serve garnished with a thinly sliced orange.

Danish Apple Charlotte ⓁⓁⓁ

4 SERVINGS	Metric/UK/	US
Frozen cooking apples, sliced	675g/1½lb	1½lb
Grated zest 1 lemon		
Water	2 tablespoons	2 tbsp
Sugar	4 tablespoons	4 tbsp
Butter	125g/4oz	½ cup
White breadcrumbs	175g/6oz	2 cups
Light brown sugar	4 tablespoons	4 tbsp
DECORATION		
Double [heavy] cream, whipped	150ml/5fl oz	⅝ cup
Chocolate, coarsely grated	50g/2oz/2 squares	

Place the frozen apple slices into a saucepan with the lemon zest, water and white sugar. Cover, and cook until the apples are soft, then mash to a smooth purée. Leave to cool.

Melt the butter in a large frying pan and gently fry the breadcrumbs until crisp and golden. Add the brown sugar and allow to cool.

Line a serving dish with foil, leaving enough foil overlapping to cover the top. Put half the apple purée into the bottom of the foil lined dish, add half the crumbs and then the remaining apple purée and top with the rest of the crumbs.

To freeze: Fold the overlapping foil to cover the top of the dish. Seal, label and freeze. When firm remove the foil parcel from the dish and place in a polythene [plastic] bag.

To serve: Unwrap the frozen charlotte and replace in the serving dish. Thaw in the refrigerator for 12 hours. Spread the lightly whipped cream over the top, and sprinkle on the grated chocolate.

Avocado Ice-Cream Ⓛ

600ml (1 pint) [2½ cups]	Metric/UK	US
Ripe avocados, halved and stoned	4/4	4
Juice of 1 lemon		
3 drops green food colouring		
Double cream [heavy cream]	250ml/8fl oz	1 cup
Sour cream	250ml/8fl oz	1 cup
Vanilla pod	1/1	1
Egg yolks	3/3	3
Sugar	50g/2oz	¼ cup
Water	75ml/3fl oz	⅜ cup
Egg whites, stiffly beaten	3/3	3

Using a teaspoon, scoop the flesh from the avocados and place it in a small mixing bowl. Pour the lemon juice into the bowl. Using a fork, mash the avocado flesh with the lemon juice and green food colouring until it forms a smooth paste. Set aside.

Place the cream and sour cream in a medium-sized saucepan. Set the pan over low heat and scald the cream (bring to just under boiling point). Remove the pan from the heat. Add the vanilla pod to the pan, cover it and set aside for 20 minutes.

Strain the cream into a small mixing bowl. Remove and discard the vanilla pod. Set the cream aside.

In a medium-sized mixing bowl, beat the egg yolks with a wire whisk or rotary beater until they are pale. Set aside.

In a small saucepan, dissolve the sugar in the water over low heat, stirring constantly. When the sugar has dissolved, increase the heat to moderate and boil the syrup until the temperature reaches 100°C (220°F) on a sugar thermometer or until a little of the syrup dropped into cold water forms a short thread when drawn out between your index finger and thumb. Remove the pan from the heat and let the syrup cool for 1 minute.

Pour the syrup on to the egg yolks in a steady stream, whisking constantly with a wire whisk or rotary beater. Continue whisking until the mixture is thick and fluffy. Using a metal spoon, gently but thoroughly fold in the avocado mixture. Stir in the cooled cream. With the metal spoon, fold in the egg whites.

To freeze: Pour the mixture into an ice-cream container. Seal, label and freeze.

To serve: Spoon the ice-cream into individual dishes and serve with a lemon sauce.

Black Cherry Tart ⓁⓁ

8 SERVINGS	Metric/UK/	US
Rich shortcrust pastry, thawed	350g/12oz	3 cups
Canned stoned black cherries	450g/1lb	1lb
Gelatine	25g/1oz	1oz
Brandy	4 tablespoons	4 tbsp
Double [heavy] cream	250ml/8fl oz	1 cup

Heat oven to 200°C (Gas Mark 6, 400°F).

Roll out the pastry and line a well-buttered 30cm (12 inch) fluted flan case.

Bake blind for 20-25 minutes, then take out and cool on a wire rack.

Drain the cherries and reserve the juice.

Soak the gelatine for 5 minutes in the cherry juice before dissolving over a low heat. Set aside to cool and then mix with the brandy.

Beat the cream until stiff and spoon on to the bottom of the cold pastry case, reserving a little of the cream for decoration. Neatly arrange the cherries on top.

Brush the cherries with the almost set juice.

Decorate with rosettes of whipped cream.

To freeze: Freeze free-flow. When firm pack carefully into a rigid container to avoid damaging the decoration. Seal and label.

To serve: Thaw in the refrigerator for 12 hours.

Crêpes Suzette ⓁⓁⓁ

4 SERVINGS	Metric/UK/	US
Rich pancake [crêpe] batter	300ml/½ pint	1¼ cups
Unsalted butter	75g/3oz	⅜ cup
Sugar	125g/4oz	½ cup
Finely grated orange zest	2 teaspoons	2 tsp
Juice of half an orange		
Cointreau or Curaçao	2 tablespoons	2 tbsp
Brandy or rum	2 tablespoons	2 tbsp

Cook 8-10 thin pancakes [crêpes] from the batter.

To freeze: Cool each pancake [crêpe] taking care not to damage. When completely cold stack the pancakes [crêpes], interleaving each with 2 sheets of greaseproof or waxed paper. Place the package into a rigid container. Seal, label and freeze.

To serve: Preheat the oven to 130°C (Gas Mark ½, 250°F). Thaw the pancakes [crêpes] in the oven for 5-10 minutes. Meanwhile, heat the butter, sugar, orange zest and juice in a large frying pan, or heatproof dish, over a gentle heat until the sugar has dissolved. Add the Cointreau or Curaçao. Fold each thawed pancake [crêpe] into four. Put them into the pan and heat through gently in the sauce, turning twice. Decorate with

orange slices, pour on the brandy, and then flame the pancakes. Serve at once.

Note: It is best to use a long taper to light the brandy. Do not allow the sauce to heat for long after the brandy is added, or the flames may flare too high.

Above: Use your freezer to cut down on the preparations of Crêpes Suzette and cook this dish at your leisure at the table.

25

Cold food

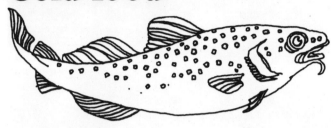

Taramasalata   ⓛ ⓛ

6 SERVINGS	Metric/UK/	US
Smoked cod's roe, thawed and skinned	450g/1lb	1lb
White bread, crusts removed and soaked in milk for 15 minutes	4 slices 4 slices	4 slices
Garlic cloves, crushed	4/4	4
Olive oil	300ml/10fl oz	1¼ cups
Lemon juice	4 tablespoons	4 tbsp
Freshly ground black pepper	½ teaspoon	½ tsp
GARNISH		
Cucumber, thinly sliced	¼/¼	¼
Firm tomatoes, sliced	6/6	6
Black olives	6/6	6

Place the cod's roe in a large mixing bowl and pound it with the end of a rolling pin, or use a pestle and mortar, until the gritty texture is eliminated.

Squeeze as much moisture out of the bread as possible and add it to the bowl, with the garlic. Continue pounding until the mixture is smooth.

Add the oil, a few drops at a time, pounding constantly and adding a little of the lemon juice from time to time. Continue pounding until the mixture forms a soft, smooth paste and is pale pink in colour.

Alternatively, place all the ingredients in the jar of an electric blender and blend at moderately high speed until a soft paste is formed.

Beat the pepper into the mixture.

To freeze: Place the taramasalata in a rigid container. Seal, label and freeze.

To serve: Thaw in the refrigerator for 12 hours. Arrange equal quantities of the taramasalata on 6 small serving plates. Surround the paste with the cucumber and tomato slices and top each portion with an olive. Serve with hot toast.

Below: Taramasalata is a Greek dish and makes a delicious start to a meal especially if served with hot Pita (Greek bread).

Courgette [Zucchini] and Tomato Quiche

4-6 SERVINGS	Metric/UK/	US
Uncooked frozen flan case made with shortcrust pastry	1x23cm/1x9 inch	
FILLING		
Butter	50g/2oz	¼ cup
Garlic cloves, crushed	2/2	2
Frozen courgettes [zucchini], sliced	225g/8oz	8oz
Salt	1 teaspoon	1 tsp
Black pepper	1 teaspoon	1 tsp
Dried oregano	½ teaspoon	½ tsp
Single cream [light cream]	125ml/4fl oz	½ cup
Eggs	3/3	3
Cheddar cheese, grated	50g/2oz	½ cup
Small tomatoes, thawed, peeled and thinly sliced	5/5	5

Preheat the oven to fairly hot 200°C (Gas Mark 6, 400°F). Place the flan case on a baking sheet and set aside.

In a large frying pan, melt the butter over moderate heat. When the foam subsides, add the garlic and cook, stirring frequently, for 1 minute. Add the courgettes (zucchini) and half of the salt and pepper. Cook, stirring and turning occasionally, for 8-10 minutes or until the courgettes [zucchini] are lightly browned. Remove the pan from the heat and stir in the remaining salt and pepper and the oregano, mixing well to blend.

In a medium-sized mixing bowl, combine the cream, eggs and grated cheese and beat well to blend.

Arrange the courgettes [zucchini] and tomato slices in concentric circles in the flan case.

Pour the cream mixture over the courgettes [zucchini] and tomatoes.

Place the baking sheet in the centre of the oven and bake the quiche for 35-40 minutes or until the filling is set and firm and golden brown on top.

To freeze: Cool. Freeze free-flow. When firm close wrap in foil, taking care not to damage the flan case. Place the foil package in a rigid container. Seal and label.

To serve: Thaw in the refrigerator for 12 hours and serve with garlic bread and tossed green salad. Ⓛ Ⓛ

Iced Carrot Soup Ⓛ Ⓛ

8 SERVINGS	Metric/UK/	US
Frozen carrots, sliced	450g/1lb	1lb
Frozen cut celery	175g/6oz	6oz
Frozen onion, sliced	75g/3oz	3oz
Bayleaf	1/1	1
Salt	½ teaspoon	½ tsp
White pepper	½ teaspoon	½ tsp
Cloves	2/2	2
Chicken stock made from stock cubes	900ml/1½pints	3¾cups
Chopped parsley	2 tablespoons	2 tbsp
GARNISH		
Single [light] cream	125ml/4fl oz	½ cup

In a large saucepan combine the carrots, celery, onion, seasoning and chicken stock. Bring to the boil, then simmer over a moderate heat until the vegetables are quite soft.

Remove the pan from the stove and pour the contents through a strainer into a large bowl. Press the vegetables through the strainer with a wooden spoon, or use a food mill.

Stir in the chopped parsley.

To freeze: Cool. Pour the soup into a rigid container. Seal, label and freeze.

To serve: Thaw in the refrigerator for 12 hours. When thawed stir in the cream, adjust the seasoning and serve with croûtons.

Chicken Liver and Bacon Pâté Ⓛ Ⓛ

4-6 SERVINGS	Metric/UK/	US
Chicken liver, thawed	125g/¼lb	¼lb
Fatty bacon, thawed, de-rinded	125g/¼lb	¼lb
Frozen onion, chopped	75g/3oz	3oz
Clove of garlic, crushed	1/1	1
Butter	65g/2½oz	5 tbsp
Milk	150ml/5fl oz	⅝ cup
Blade mace (or a good pinch of ground mace)	1/1	1
Bay leaf	1/1	1
Peppercorns	2-3/2-3	2-3
Flour	15g/½oz	1 tbsp
Anchovy essence [extract]	½ teaspoon	½ tsp
Prepared mustard	1 teaspoon	1 tsp
Salt and pepper		

Heat oven to 180°C (Gas Mark 4, 350°F).

Gently fry the liver, bacon, onion and garlic in 57g (2oz) [¼ cup] of the butter for about 10 minutes. Remove from the heat, and either purée in a blender or mince [grind]. Put the milk into a saucepan with the mace, bay leaf and peppercorns. Bring slowly to the boil, remove from the heat, and leave for 5 minutes. Melt the remaining butter in a saucepan, add the flour and cook for 1 minute.

Gradually add the strained milk and bring to the boil, stirring all the time until it thickens. Remove from the heat and stir in the meat mixture, anchovy essence [extract] and mustard. Season to taste. Turn into a small, well-greased terrine and cover with a lid or foil. Stand in a roasting tin containing 3cm (1 inch) of cold water and bake in a moderate oven for 1 hour.

To freeze: Cool. Cover the terrine with foil. Seal, label and freeze.

To serve: Thaw in the refrigerator for 12 hours and serve from the terrine with hot buttered toast.

Beef Loaf   Ⓛ Ⓛ Ⓛ

6-8 SERVINGS	Metric/UK/	US
Lean minced [ground] beef, thawed	1.35kg [approx] 3lb	
Bacon, thawed, rind removed and cut into small pieces	4 slices/4 slices	
		4 slices
Dried thyme	1 teaspoon	1 tsp
Salt	2 teaspoons	2 tsp
Freshly ground black pepper	$\frac{1}{2}$ teaspoon	$\frac{1}{2}$ tsp
Garlic clove, crushed	1/1	1
Red wine	4 tablespoons	4 tbsp
Wine vinegar	1 tablespoon	1 tbsp
French mustard	1 teaspoon	1 tsp
Vegetable oil	1 tablespoon	1 tbsp

Put the beef, bacon, thyme, salt, pepper, garlic, wine, vinegar and mustard in a large bowl and mix them well. Put the bowl into the refrigerator, cover and leave for at least 2 hours.

Preheat the oven to warm 170°C (Gas Mark 3, 325°F).

Using a pastry brush, grease a 1kg (2lb) loaf tin with the vegetable oil. Put the meat mixture into the tin.

Put the filled loaf tin into a large baking pan and half-fill the pan with water. Place the pan in the centre of the oven and cook the meat loaf for 1½ hours. After 1 hour, cover the loaf tin with foil to prevent the meat from becoming too dry.

Remove the meat loaf from the oven and leave it to cool for at least one hour. Unmould it by running a knife around the edges of the tin and turning it out on to a plate.

To freeze: Close wrap the meat loaf in foil and place in a polythene [plastic] bag. Seal, label and freeze.

To serve: Thaw in the refrigerator for 24 hours.

Below: Sandwiches can be made up in the normal way and frozen. The variations on fillings are endless but do avoid using hard boiled eggs, salad vegetables, mayonnaise or tomatoes, as these do not freeze well. Thaw packs of sandwiches at room temperature for 2½-3 hours, or spread out on a plate for 1 hour. Do not store sandwiches in the freezer for longer than 2 months.

Above: Beef Loaf, and Right: Veal and Ham Pie, make ideal picnic meals in the summer.

Veal and Ham Pie   Ⓛ Ⓛ Ⓛ

4-6 SERVINGS	Metric/UK/	US
Stewing veal, thawed	450g/1lb	1lb
Lean bacon, thawed	225g/$\frac{1}{2}$lb	$\frac{1}{2}$lb
Chopped parsley	1 tablespoon	1 tbsp
Grated nutmeg	$\frac{1}{4}$ teaspoon	$\frac{1}{4}$ tsp
Salt and pepper		
Hot water crust pastry	350g/12oz	3 cups
Beaten egg to glaze		
Powdered gelatine	2 teaspoons	2 tsps
Stock	150ml/5fl oz	$\frac{5}{8}$ cup

Heat oven to 200°C (Gas Mark 6, 400°F).

Chop the veal and bacon, then blend in the parsley, nutmeg and seasoning. Make up the pastry. Using two-thirds of the pastry, mould it around the inside of a 15cm (6 inch) diameter loose-bottomed cake tin. Put the filling into the tin.

Pat the rest of the pastry out to a circle for the lid. Place this on top and pinch the edges together to seal, trimming off any excess pastry. Make a slit in the top of the pie for the steam to escape.

Bake the pie for 10 minutes, then lower the heat to warm 170°C (Gas Mark 3, 325°F) and cook for a further 2¼ hours. Half-way through cooking, remove the pie from the cake tin and brush all over with beaten egg.

Allow the baked pie to cool. Soften the gelatine in the stock, then put in a bowl over a pan of gently simmering water until dissolved. Allow to cool, but not to set. Carefully pour the cool gelatine mixture through the hole in the top.

To freeze: Close wrap the pie in foil and place in a polythene [plastic] bag. Seal, label and freeze.

To serve: Thaw in the refrigerator for 24 hours and serve cut in wedges like a cake with a crisp green salad.

Mutton Pies ⓁⓁⓁ

15 PIES	Metric/UK/	US
Frozen leg mutton, thawed and boned	450g/1lb	1lb
Salt	1½ teaspoons	1½ tsp
Bouquet garni, consisting of 4 parsley sprigs, 1 thyme spray and 1 bay leaf tied together		
Frozen whole medium-sized onions	2/2	2
Butter	1 tablespoon	1 tbsp
Frozen onion, finely chopped	225g/8oz	8oz
Frozen carrot, finely chopped	50g/2oz	2oz
Frozen turnip, finely chopped	175g/6oz	6oz
Chicken stock	150ml/5fl oz	⅝ cup
Hot water crust pastry dough	225g/8oz	2 cups
Black pepper	½ teaspoon	½ tsp
Chopped fresh parsley	1 tablespoon	1 tbsp
Egg, lightly beaten	1/1	1

Place the mutton in a large saucepan. Pour in enough water just to cover and add 1 teaspoon of salt, the bouquet garni and the two whole onions. Place the pan over moderately high heat and bring the water to the boil, skimming off any scum that rises to the surface. Reduce the heat to low, cover the pan and simmer the mutton for 1-1¼ hours or until it is tender when pierced with the point of a sharp knife.

Remove the pan from the heat and allow the mutton to cool in the cooking liquid. When the mutton has cooled, skim off any fat that has formed on the surface of the liquid. Using two large spoons, lift the meat out of the pan and place it on a chopping board. Discard the cooking liquid and vegetables.

With a sharp knife, cut the mutton into very small pieces.

Place them in a large mixing bowl.

Preheat the oven to hot 220°C (Gas Mark 7, 425°F). With the tablespoon of butter, lightly grease 15 patty tins and set them aside.

Place the chopped onion, carrot and turnip in a small saucepan and pour over the chicken stock. Place the pan over moderate heat and cook the vegetables for 10 minutes or until they are tender.

Meanwhile, divide the dough in half and set one half aside. On a lightly floured surface, roll out the other half to a circle about 6mm (¼ inch) thick. With a 8cm (3 inch) pastry cutter, cut the dough into 15 circles. Line the prepared patty tins with the circles.

Roll out the remaining dough to a circle about 6mm (¼ inch) thick and, using a 5cm (2 inch) pastry cutter, cut the dough into 15 circles. Set the circles aside.

Remove the pan containing the vegetables from the heat and drain the vegetables, reserving the cooking liquid. Add the vegetables to the meat, then add the remaining salt, the pepper, parsley and enough of the reserved liquid to moisten the mixture. Stir well to blend.

Spoon the mixture into the prepared patty tins and cover with the reserved dough circles, crimping the dough together at the edges to seal. With a sharp knife, cut a small slit in the tops. With a pastry brush, brush the tops of the pies with the beaten egg.

Place the patty tins in the oven and bake the pies for 20-30 minutes or until the pastry is golden brown. Remove the pies from the oven and let them cool slightly in the patty tins. Carefully remove the pies from the tins and place them on a wire rack.

To freeze: Cool completely. Freeze free-flow. When firm pack the pies into a rigid container. Seal and label.

To serve: Thaw in the refrigerator for 12 hours and serve with a mixed green salad.

Cold Lemon and Honey Duck Ⓛ Ⓛ

4-5 SERVINGS	Metric/UK/	US
Duck, thawed	1.75kg- 1x4-4½lb	
Salt and pepper	2kg [approx]	
Lemon	1/1	1
Clear honey	3 tablespoons	3 tbsp
Olive oil	50ml/2fl oz	¼ cup
STUFFING		
Fresh breadcrumbs	150g/5oz	2½ cups
Chopped nuts	50g/2oz	½ cup
Seedless raisins	75g/3oz	½ cup
Frozen onion, chopped	75g/3oz	3oz
Dried thyme	1 teaspoon	1 tsp
Grated zest of lemon	2 teaspoons	2 tsp
Salt and pepper		
Egg, beaten	1/1	1
Milk	50ml/2fl oz	¼ cup

Left: Mutton Pies are time-consuming to make, but save time by making a large batch and freezing.
Below: Cold Lemon and Honey Duck.

Make several small incisions in the duck flesh with a sharp knife, and rub the duck all over with salt and pepper.

Squeeze the lemon and mix the juice with 2 tablespoons of honey and the olive oil. Using your hands, rub the mixture all over the duck.

Place the duck in a large mixing bowl, cover lightly with a cloth, and leave in a cool place for 24 hours, basting occasionally with the mixture.

Next day, heat the oven to 180°C (Gas Mark 4, 350°F).

Tip into a small mixing bowl all the dry ingredients for the stuffing. Mix well then bind together with the egg and milk.

Stuff the duck with the mixture, wrap it loosely in aluminium foil, place on a roasting tray and cook for 1 hour 40 minutes. At regular intervals unwrap the foil and baste the duck with its juices.

Then completely unwrap the foil, carefully spoon the remaining tablespoon of honey over the duck, and continue cooking, uncovered, for 20 minutes, basting at least once.

To freeze: Cool completely. Close wrap the duck in foil and place in a polythene [plastic] bag. Seal, label and freeze.

To serve: Thaw in the refrigerator for 24 hours. Place on a serving dish and garnish with slices of lemon and watercress.

Apricot Bourdaloue Tart ⓛ ⓛ

4 to 6 SERVINGS	Metric/UK/	US
PASTRY		
Flour	125g/4oz	**1 cup**
A pinch of salt		
Castor [superfine] **sugar**	2 teaspoons	2 tsp
Butter	2 tablespoons	2 tbsp
Vegetable shortening	2 tablespoons	2 tbsp
Egg yolk	1/1	1
Iced water	$\frac{1}{2}$-1tablespoon	$\frac{1}{2}$-1tbsp
FILLING		
Egg yolks	2/2	2
Egg white	1/1	1
Castor [superfine] **sugar**	50g/2oz	$\frac{1}{4}$ **cup**
Grated rind of 1 orange		
Cornflour [cornstarch]	1$\frac{1}{2}$ tablespoons	1$\frac{1}{2}$ tbsp
Flour	1$\frac{1}{2}$ tablespoons	1$\frac{1}{2}$ tbsp
Milk	300ml/10fl oz	1$\frac{1}{4}$ **cups**
Canned halved apricots, or frozen	425ml/14oz	14oz
apricots halves, poached in syrup	450g/1lb	1lb
DECORATION		
Roasted almonds, flaked	25g/1oz	$\frac{1}{4}$ **cup**

Preheat oven to moderate 180°C (Gas Mark 4, 350°F).

Sift the flour and salt into a medium-sized mixing bowl. Add the sugar and mix. Using a table knife, cut the butter and vegetable shortening into the flour. Using your fingertips, rub the fat into the flour until the mixture resembles fine breadcrumbs. Make a well in the centre of the mixture and add the egg yolk mixed with $\frac{1}{2}$ tablespoon of iced water. To begin with, use the knife to mix the flour mixture with the egg yolk, then use your hands to knead the pastry until it is smooth. Add more iced water if the pastry is too dry. Pat the pastry into a ball, cover and refrigerate for 15 minutes.

Roll out the pastry to line a 19cm (7$\frac{1}{2}$ inch) flan tin. Refrigerate for 10 minutes. Bake blind, covering the bottom with foil weighed down with dried beans, for 30 minutes.

To make the crème bourdaloue, in a medium-sized mixing bowl beat egg yolks with half the sugar. Add the grated orange rind, the cornflour and the flour and beat until smooth. Put the milk in a pan on moderate heat and bring to the boil. Just as it comes to the boil, pour it slowly, stirring all the time, over the egg mixture. Stir until smooth. Return the mixture to the pan and, stirring constantly, bring to the boil. Remove from the heat and cool.

In a small mixing bowl, beat the white of the egg with remaining sugar until stiff. Fold it into the cooked mixture.

Drain the apricot halves. Put the syrup into a small pan and boil rapidly until it thickens. Cool and set aside.

Remove the pastry shell from the tin and place it on a serving dish. Put the crème bourdaloue into the middle of the pastry shell and smooth with a knife into a shallow rounded shape. Cover the crème completely with the apricots and brush over with the reduced syrup.

To freeze: Freeze free-flow. When firm close wrap the tart in foil, taking care to avoid damage to the flan case. Place the foil package in a rigid container. Seal and label.

To serve: Thaw in the refrigerator for 12 hours and decorate with flaked almonds.

Gingerbread

(L)(L)

ABOUT 2kg [2lb] BREAD	Metric/UK/	US
Butter	75g/3oz	⅜ cup
Butter	1 teaspoon	1 tsp
Flour	225g/8oz	2 cups
Bicarbonate of soda [baking soda]	½ teaspoon	½ tsp
Ground ginger	1½ teaspoons	1½ tsp
Ground cloves	¼ teaspoon	¼ tsp
Ground cinnamon	½ teaspoon	½ tsp
Salt	¼ teaspoon	¼ tsp
Sugar	125g/4oz	½ cup
Egg	1/1	1
Treacle [molasses]	175g/6fl oz	¾ cup
Sour cream	225g/8fl oz	1 cup
Raisins	50g/2oz	⅓ cup

Preheat the oven to moderate 180°C (Gas Mark 4, 350°F). Lightly grease a 24 x 14 x 6cm (9½ x 5½ x 2½ inch) loaf tin with the teaspoon of butter. Set aside.

Sift the flour, soda, ginger, cloves, cinnamon and salt into a medium-sized mixing bowl. Set aside.

In a large mixing bowl, cream the remaining butter and the sugar together with a wooden spoon until the mixture is light and fluffy. Add the egg and treacle [molasses] and beat until the mixture is smooth. Stir in the sour cream.

Gradually incorporate the flour mixture into the butter-and-sugar mixture, beating constantly until the mixture is smooth. Stir in the raisins.

Pour the mixture into the greased loaf tin and place the tin in the oven. Bake the gingerbread for 1¼ hours, or until a skewer inserted into the centre of the bread comes out clean.

Remove the gingerbread from the oven and allow it to cool a little in the tin. Run the tip of a sharp knife lightly around the edge of the gingerbread and gently ease it out of the tin on to a wire cake rack.

To freeze: Cool completely. Close wrap the gingerbread in foil and place in a polythene [plastic] bag. Seal, label and freeze.

To serve: Thaw in the refrigerator for 24 hours.

Left: Gingerbread is both simple to make and a delicious addition to any picnic, as well as a coffee break or tea-time treat.

Orange and Lemon Flan

(L)(L)(L)

6-8 SERVINGS	Metric/UK/	US
Pre-baked pastry tart shell	1x23cm/	1x9 inch
FILLING		
Eggs	2/2	2
Castor [superfine] sugar	75g/3oz	⅜ cup
Single [light] cream	125ml/4fl oz	½ cup
Stale cake crumbs	125g/4oz	1 cup
The grated zest and juice of 1 small orange		
A few drops of almond essence [extract]		
TOPPING		
Large thin-skinned lemons	2/2	2
Small thin-skinned oranges	2/2	2
Water	150ml/5fl oz	⅝ cup
Sugar	75g/3oz	⅜ cup
Sieved marmalade	4 tablespoons	4 tbsp

Heat the oven to 190°C (Gas Mark 5, 375°F).

Prepare the filling by whisking the eggs with the sugar until thick and creamy. Add the remaining ingredients and beat vigorously until well mixed.

Spread the mixture in the flan shell and bake for 30-40 minutes or until well risen, golden, and firm to the touch in the centre.

Meanwhile prepare the topping by slicing the oranges and lemons very thinly, removing all the pips [seeds]. If the pith on the fruit is thick, peel them with a sharp knife, as you would an apple, or they may be rather bitter.

Dissolve the sugar in the water in a shallow, wide pan and bring to the boil.

Lay the orange and lemon slices in the syrup and simmer for 3 minutes, then remove and drain well.

Boil the remaining syrup until reduced by half. Stir in the marmalade and heat until it is completely melted to give a good, rich glaze.

Arrange the orange and lemon slices on top of the tart and brush generously with the glaze.

To freeze: Cool. Freeze free-flow. When firm wrap carefully in foil, avoiding any damage to the flan case. Place the foil package in a rigid container. Seal and label.

To serve: Thaw in the refrigerator for 12 hours. Place the tart under a hot grill [broiler] for a few minutes until the glaze is bubbling and caramelized.

Serve cold, decorated with pieces of glacé cherries if wished, and an accompanying jug of cream.

Quick meals

Scampi Provençale　Ⓛ

4 SERVINGS	Metric/UK/	US
Butter, or	25g/1oz	2 tbsp
Olive oil	2 tablespoons	2 tbsp
Frozen onion, chopped	125g/4oz	4oz
Clove garlic, crushed	1/1	1
Tomatoes, thawed	450g/1lb	1lb
Dry sherry	1 tablespoon	1 tbsp
Chopped parsley	1 tablespoon	1 tbsp
Salt and pepper		
Frozen cooked scampi [shrimp]	225g/½lb	½lb

Heat the butter, or oil, in a pan. Add the onion and garlic and cook gently for about 10 minutes or until the onion is soft. Peel the tomatoes, cut into quarters and remove the seeds. Add to the pan with the sherry, parsley, scampi and seasoning. Cover and cook for 10 minutes.

To freeze: Cool. Place provençale in a small rigid container. Seal, label and freeze.

To serve: Thaw over a gentle heat, stirring frequently until completely heated. Serve with crusty french bread.

Italian Meat and Vegetable Soup　ⓁⓁⓁ

4 SERVINGS	Metric/UK/	US
Butter	50g/2oz	¼ cup
Vegetable oil	2 tablespoons	2 tbsp
Frozen onion, finely chopped	175g/6oz	6oz
Garlic clove, chopped	1/1	1
Minced [ground] beef, thawed	450g/1lb	1lb
Beef stock	1.75ltr/3pt	7½ cups
Salt	2 teaspoons	2 tsp
Black pepper	½ teaspoon	½ tsp
Dried oregano	1 teaspoon	1 tsp
Dried basil	½ teaspoon	½ tsp
Frozen courgettes [zucchini], sliced	175g/6oz	6oz
Frozen peas	125g/4oz	4oz
Canned peeled tomatoes, drained and coarsely chopped	125g/4oz	4oz

In a large saucepan, melt the butter with the oil over moderate heat. When the foam subsides, add the onion and garlic and fry them, stirring occasionally, for 6-8 minutes, or until the onion is golden brown.

Add the beef and fry, stirring occasionally, for 8 minutes, or until the meat is broken up and browned.

Pour in the stock and add the salt, pepper, oregano, basil, courgettes [zucchini] and peas and bring to the boil. Reduce the heat to low and simmer for 15 minutes.

Add the tomatoes and simmer for a further 5 minutes.

To freeze: Cool. Pour the soup into 2 rigid containers leaving 1cm (½ inch) head space. Seal, label and freeze.

To serve: Thaw over a low heat, stirring frequently until completely heated. Remove the pan from the heat and pour the soup into a warmed soup tureen. Sprinkle the soup with grated Parmesan cheese.

Above: Rich, simple to make Scampi Provençale. Right: Racuchy is an unusual starter. Below: Italian Meat and Vegetable Soup is almost a meal in itself.

Racuchy

(L)(L)(L)

4-6 SERVINGS	Metric/UK/	US
Large potatoes, peeled and finely grated	4/4	4
Frozen onion, very finely chopped	75g/3oz	3oz
Egg yolk	1/1	1
Flour	1 tablespoon	1 tbsp
Dried oregano	$\frac{1}{4}$ teaspoon	$\frac{1}{4}$ tsp
Chopped fresh chives	1 tablespoon	1 tbsp
Salt	1 teaspoon	1 tsp
Freshly ground black pepper	$\frac{1}{2}$ teaspoon	$\frac{1}{2}$ tsp
Egg white, stiffly whipped	1/1	1
Sufficient vegetable oil for deep-drying		

Place the potatoes, onion, egg yolk, flour, oregano, chives, salt and pepper in a large mixing bowl. Stir the ingredients with a wooden spoon until they are thoroughly combined.

Using a metal spoon, fold the beaten egg white into the potato mixture. Set aside.

Fill a deep-frying pan one-third full with vegetable oil. Place the pan over moderate heat and heat the oil until it registers 190°C (375°F) on a deep-fat thermometer, or until a small cube of stale bread dropped into the oil turns golden brown in 40 seconds.

Carefully drop 3 or 4 tablespoons of the potato mixture into the oil and fry them for 1-2 minutes, do not let them brown.

With a slotted spoon, remove the racuchy from the oil and drain them on kitchen paper towels.

To freeze: Cool. Freeze free-flow. When firm pack into a polythene [plastic] bag. Seal and label.

To serve: Heat the oil to 182°C (360°F). Drop the frozen racuchy into the hot oil and fry them for 2-3 minutes or until they are crisp and golden brown. Remove the racuchy with a slotted spoon and drain on absorbent paper. Serve hot with slices of Polish salami.

Stuffed Mushrooms

(L)(L)

4 SERVINGS	Metric/UK/	US
Large mushrooms, wiped	12/12	12
Salt	1 teaspoon	1 tsp
Freshly ground black pepper	$\frac{1}{2}$ teaspoon	$\frac{1}{2}$ tsp
Melted butter	1 tablespoon	1 tbsp
Butter	2 tablespoons	2 tbsp
Shallots or spring onions [scallions], finely chopped	2/2	2
Flour	1 tablespoon	1 tbsp
Single cream [light cream]	125g/4oz	$\frac{1}{2}$ cup
Chopped fresh parsley	3 tablespoons	3 tbsp
Grated Parmesan cheese	$1\frac{1}{2}$ tablespoons	$1\frac{1}{2}$ tbsp

Remove the stems from the mushrooms and set them aside. Season the mushroom caps with $\frac{1}{2}$ teaspoon of salt and $\frac{1}{4}$ teaspoon black pepper, and, using a pastry brush, coat them with the melted butter. Arrange them, hollow side up, in a shallow baking dish.

With a sharp knife chop the mushroom stems finely. Wrap them in kitchen paper towels and twist to extract as much juice from them as possible.

In a medium-sized frying pan melt the 2 tablespoons of butter over moderate heat.

When the foam subsides, add the chopped mushroom stems and shallots or spring onions [scallions]. Sauté them together for 4-5 minutes. Reduce the heat to low and, stirring constantly, add the flour. Cook for 1 minute.

Remove the pan from the heat and stir in the cream, a little at a time. When the sauce is smooth and all the ingredients are blended, return the pan to the heat and simmer the sauce for 2-3 minutes, or until it has thickened.

Stir in the parsley and the remaining salt and pepper and mix well.

Remove the pan from the heat and spoon a little of the mixture into each of the prepared mushroom caps.

Top each mushroom with a little grated cheese.

To freeze: Freeze free-flow. When firm pack the mushrooms into a rigid container. Seal and label.

To serve: Preheat the oven to 180°C (Gas Mark 4, 350°F). Place the frozen mushrooms on a heatproof serving dish and bake the mushrooms in the oven for 25-30 minutes or until they are tender and the stuffing is lightly browned on top.

Remove from the oven and serve.

Danish Meat Balls   Ⓛ Ⓛ Ⓛ

4-6 SERVINGS	Metric/UK/	US
Minced [ground] beef, thawed	350g/12oz	12oz
Minced [ground] pork, thawed	350g/12oz	12oz
Flour	3 tablespoons	3 tbsp
Salt	½ teaspoon	½ tsp
Freshly milled black pepper		
Ground allspice	¼ teaspoon	¼ tsp
Frozen onion, finely chopped	75g/3oz	3oz
Milk	150ml/5fl oz	⅝ cup
Egg, beaten	1/1	1
Butter	4 tablespoons	¼ cup
Oil	1 tablespoon	1 tbsp

Mix the meat with the flour, salt, pepper, allspice and onion. Gradually beat in the milk and egg.

Using two tablespoons, shape the mixture into oval balls. Heat the butter and oil in a frying pan, and fry the meat balls gently on all sides until they are golden brown.

To freeze: Cool. Freeze free-flow. When firm pack the meat balls in a polythene [plastic] bag. Seal and label.

To serve: Preheat the oven to 180°C (Gas Mark 4, 350°F). Transfer the frozen meat balls to an ovenproof dish and thaw in the oven for 15-20 minutes until completely heated. Serve with duchess potatoes and red cabbage.

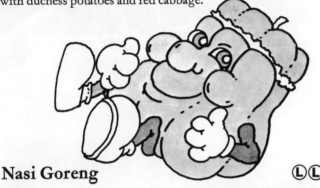

Nasi Goreng   Ⓛ Ⓛ

4 SERVINGS	Metric/UK/	US
Long grain rice	350g/12oz	2 cups
Frozen mixed vegetables	450g/1lb	1lb
Shoulder of pork, thawed	575g/1¼lb	1¼lb
Frozen onions, sliced	450g/1lb	1lb
Butter or margarine	125g/4oz	½ cup
Soy sauce	3 tablespoons	3 tbsp
Mild curry powder	1½ teaspoons	1½ tsp
Salt and pepper		

Cook the rice in boiling salted water for 12 minutes. Drain, and rinse under cold water to remove all the surplus starch. Drain again. Cook the mixed vegetables in boiling salted water following the instructions on the packet. Drain well. Cut the pork into cubes.

Heat half the butter in a large pan and fry the onions and pork for about 20 minutes over a medium heat. Turn from time to time. Add the remaining butter, the rice, mixed vegetables, soy sauce, curry powder and seasoning and mix well.

To freeze: Cool. Transfer the Nasi Goreng to a rigid container. Seal, label and freeze.

To serve: Thaw very gently over a low heat, stirring frequently. Serve hot with a green salad, peanuts and shrimp crisps [chips].

Paella   Ⓛ

4 SERVINGS	Metric/UK/	US
Frozen onion, chopped	125g/4oz	4oz
Clove of garlic	1/1	1
Oil	5 tablespoons	5 tbsp
Long-grain rice	350g/12oz	2 cups
Chicken stock, heated	600ml/1 pint	2½ cups
Cooked chicken	350g/12oz	12oz
Tinned sweet red pimiento	1/1	1
Frozen mussels, or	175g/6oz	6oz
Can mussels, drained	1/1	1
Saffron	¼ teaspoon	¼ tsp
Frozen shrimps or prawns	225g/8oz	8oz
Frozen green peas	225g/8oz	8oz
Small jar stuffed olives	1/1	1
Salt and pepper		

Fry the onion and garlic in the hot oil until they are transparent. Add the rice and cook for 3-5 minutes. Pour in the hot chicken stock, cover with a lid and cook the rice until it is almost tender for about 7-10 minutes, adding a little more stock if necessary.

When the rice is almost cooked stir in the chicken meat, the frozen or drained mussels, sliced pimiento, saffron, shrimps or prawns and peas and stuffed olives. Season to taste.

To freeze: Cool. Place the Paella in a rigid container. Seal, label and freeze.

To serve: Reheat very gently over a low heat, stirring frequently. Serve with a dry white wine.

Stuffed Peppers   Ⓛ Ⓛ

6 SERVINGS	Metric/UK/	US
Green peppers [frozen whole peppers can be used]	6/6	6
STUFFING		
Frozen onion, chopped	75g/3oz	3oz
Frozen mushrooms, sliced	125g/4oz	1 cup
Butter	2 tablespoons	2 tbsp
Tomatoes, thawed, peeled and chopped	4/4	4
Cooked brown rice	175g/6oz	1½ cups
Salt and pepper		
Chopped fresh thyme and parsley		

Cut a slice from the stem end of each pepper. Scoop out the seeds and core. Parboil the peppers in boiling water for five minutes, drain and refresh them under cold water. Set aside. Fry the onion in the melted butter until it is soft but not brown and add the mushrooms and tomatoes to it. Add the cooked rice and season carefully with salt, pepper and herbs.

Stuff the peppers with this mixture.

To freeze: Cool. Freeze free-flow. When firm pack the frozen peppers into a rigid container. Seal and label.

To serve: Preheat the oven to 180°C (Gas Mark 4, 350°F). Transfer the frozen peppers to a well-buttered deep heatproof dish. Carefully spoon over 3dl (½ pint) [1¼ cups] stock. Cook in the oven for about 30-40 minutes, basting frequently. Serve with buttered noodles.

Add interest to a meal by serving easy-to-prepare Stuffed Peppers, either as a starter or a main course.

Knickerbocker Glory

4 SERVINGS	Metric/UK/	US
Fresh peaches, peeled	4/4	4
Fresh strawberries, washed and hulled	225g/8oz	8oz
Vanilla ice-cream	250ml/8fl oz	1 cup
Chocolate ice-cream	250ml/8fl oz	1 cup
Chocolate sauce	4 tablespoons	4 tbsp
Double cream [heavy cream]	150ml/5fl oz	$\frac{5}{8}$ cup
Large cherries	4/4	4

With a sharp knife, halve and stone [pit] the peaches, then cut them into thin slices. Set aside.

Halve the strawberries. Place one-quarter of the strawberries in each of four tall sundae glasses.

Using an ice-cream scoop or large spoon, divide the vanilla ice-cream equally among the glasses. Top with a layer of peaches. Cover the peaches with the chocolate ice-cream. Spoon over the chocolate sauce.

In a medium-sized mixing bowl, whisk the cream with a wire whisk or rotary beater until it forms stiff peaks. Divide it equally among the four glasses.

Decorate each serving with a cherry and serve at once.

Frozen Gooseberry Fool ⓁⓁ

4 SERVINGS	Metric/UK/	US
Frozen gooseberries	450g/1lb	1lb
Water	300ml/½ pint	1¼ cups
Sprig of mint		
Sugar	125g/4oz	½ cup
A little green food colouring		
Double [heavy] cream, lightly whipped	300ml/½ pint	1¼ cups

Put the frozen gooseberries in a pan with the water and mint, cover, and simmer gently for about 15 minutes until soft. Remove from the heat, stir in the sugar and a little green colouring. Discard the mint sprig. Sieve, or purée in a blender and then sieve to remove all the pips [seeds]. Allow to cool, and blend the cooled mixture with the lightly whipped cream. Turn into 4 ramekin dishes.

To freeze: Freeze free-flow. When firm wrap each dish in foil and pack together in a rigid container. Seal and label.

To serve: Allow the fool to soften in the refrigerator for 1 hour before serving. Decorate each dish with whole gooseberries.

Far left: One of the quickest desserts to prepare is using ice-cream from your freezer and fresh fruit in season, combined to make a sumptuous Knickerbocker Glory.

Left: For a sophisticated variation of Knickerbocker Glory, sprinkle Kirsch over fresh fruit cut into chunks and arrange in individual glasses with raspberry and almond water ice.

Right: Frozen Gooseberry Fool.

Noodle Pudding with Apples ⓁⓁⓁ

4-6 SERVINGS	Metric/UK/	US
Eggs	2/2	2
Milk	2 tablespoons	2 tbsp
Sugar	2 tablespoons	2 tbsp
Salt	¼ teaspoon	¼ tsp
Ground cinnamon	¼ teaspoon	¼ tsp
Ground mixed spice or allspice	¼ teaspoon	¼ tsp
Frozen cooking apples, sliced	225g/8oz	8oz
Raisins	50g/2oz	⅓ cup
Fine noodles, cooked and drained	350g/12 oz	12oz
Butter, melted	25g/1oz	2 tbsp

Preheat the oven to moderate 180°C (Gas Mark 4, 350°F).

In a large mixing bowl lightly beat the eggs with the milk and combine the sugar, salt, cinnamon, mixed spice or allspice, apples, raisins and noodles. With a wooden spoon, stir the noodle mixture until the ingredients are well mixed.

Spoon the noodle mixture into a deep foil container and pour over the melted butter.

Place the container in the oven bake for 45 minutes or until the pudding is firm to touch and lightly browned on top.

To freeze: Cool. Cover the top of the foil container with a lid. Seal, label and freeze.

To serve: Preheat the oven to 180°C (Gas Mark 4, 350°F). Place the foil container in a roasting dish and surround with 3cm (1 inch) of water and heat in the oven for 30-40 minutes.

Remove the container from the oven and serve the pudding immediately.

Apple Fritters ⓁⓁⓁ

4 SERVINGS	Metric/UK/	US
Flour	125g/4oz	1 cup
Castor [fine] sugar	2 tablespoons	2 tbsp
Egg yolks	2/2	2
Butter, melted and cooled	1 tablespoon	1 tbsp
Beer or cider	75ml/2½fl oz	5 tbsp
Water	75ml/2½fl oz	5 tbsp
Medium apples	3/3	3
Egg white	1/1	1
Deep fat for frying		

Sift the flour and sugar, make a well in the centre and add the egg yolks and the melted butter. Gradually add the liquid, mixing it all into a smooth batter and beat well.

Peel and core the apples and cut into even sized chunks. Stiffly whisk the egg white and gently fold into the batter.

Heat the deep fat—it is the correct temperature when a drop of batter immediately rises to the surface and begins to brown. Dip each apple piece into the batter and, making sure it is thoroughly coated, drop it into the hot fat and fry until it is puffed up but only pale in colour. Drain on absorbent paper.

To freeze: Cool. Freeze free-flow. When firm pack the fritters in a polythene [plastic] bag. Seal and label.

To serve: Fry the frozen fritters in deep fat until golden brown. Drain on kitchen paper and sprinkle with castor [fine] sugar. Serve with fruit purée or whipped cream flavoured with a liqueur.

Apple Fritters (left) and Rhubarb and Apple Crumble (right) are simple ways of using apples.

Rhubarb and Apple Crumble ⓁⓁⓁ

4-6 SERVINGS	Metric/UK/	US
Butter	1 teaspoon	1 tsp
Frozen rhubarb, cut	900g/2lb	2lb
Frozen cooking apples, sliced	450g/1lb	1lb
Soft brown sugar	4 tablespoons	4 tbsp
Ground cinnamon	1 teaspoon	1 tsp
TOPPING		
Flour	150g/5oz	$1\frac{1}{4}$ cups
Sugar	75g/3oz	$\frac{3}{8}$ cup
Butter	75g/3oz	$\frac{3}{8}$ cup
Ground cinnamon	$\frac{1}{2}$ teaspoon	$\frac{1}{2}$ tsp
Grated nutmeg	$\frac{1}{4}$ teaspoon	$\frac{1}{4}$ tsp

Grease a 1 litre (3 pint) [2 quart] baking dish with the teaspoon of butter.

Put the rhubarb and apples in the baking dish and sprinkle over the brown sugar and cinnamon. Set aside.

To make the crumble topping, put the flour and sugar into a medium-sized mixing bowl. Add the butter and cut it into the flour with a table knife. Using your fingertips, rub the butter into the flour and sugar until the mixture resembles coarse breadcrumbs. Mix in the cinnamon and nutmeg.

Spread the topping over the fruit to cover it completely.

To freeze: Freeze free-flow. When firm cover the top of the dish with foil and place in a polythene [plastic] bag. Seal and label.

To serve: Preheat the oven to 180°C (Gas Mark 4, 350°F). Place the frozen crumble in the oven and cook for 50-60 minutes. Serve with lots of whipped cream.

Budget cooking

Bacon and Liver Rolls   Ⓛ Ⓛ

20 ROLLS	Metric/UK/	US
Water	300ml/10fl oz	1¼ cups
Salt	½ teaspoon	½ tsp
Chicken livers, thawed	225g/8oz	8oz
Frozen onion, finely chopped	50g/2oz	2oz
Chopped parsley	2 teaspoons	2 tsp
Salt	¼ teaspoon	¼ tsp
Freshly ground black pepper		
Butter, softened	2 tablespoons	2 tbsp
Lemon juice	½ teaspoon	½ tsp
Brandy	1 teaspoon	1 tsp
Bacon slices, cut in halves	10/10	10

In a medium-sized saucepan, bring the water to the boil. Add the salt and the chicken livers. Boil them for 7 minutes or until they are just cooked. Drain the livers.

Using the back of a spoon, rub the chicken livers through a fine sieve into a bowl. Add the onions, parsley, salt, 4 grindings of pepper, butter, lemon juice and brandy. Stir the mixture well and chill it in the refrigerator for 30 minutes.

Spread the chicken liver mixture on the strips of bacon. Roll up the bacon strips and put a wooden cocktail stick through the centre of each one. Place the rolls under a fairly hot grill [broiler] and, turning them occasionally, cook them for 5 minutes.

To freeze: Cool. Freeze free-flow. When firm pack the rolls in a rigid container. Seal and label.

To serve: Place the frozen bacon rolls under a medium grill [broiler] and cook for 10 minutes or until the bacon is crisp, turning occasionally. Serve hot.

Below: Economical to make, tasty Bacon and Liver Rolls look most impressive with a simple watercress and tomato garnish. Ideal for a buffet party.

Green Pea Soup   Ⓛ Ⓛ Ⓛ

4 SERVINGS	Metric/UK/	US
Butter	25g/1oz	2 tbsp
Frozen onion, finely chopped	175g/6oz	6oz
Garlic clove, crushed	1/1	1
Chicken stock	600ml/1 pint	2½ cups
Lemon juice	1 teaspoon	1 tsp
Finely chopped fresh parsley	2 tablespoons	2 tbsp
Bay leaf	1/1	1
Frozen green peas	450g/1lb	1lb
Frozen cooked ham, diced	2 slices	2 slices	2 slices
GARNISH		
Single cream [light cream]	150ml/5fl oz	⅝ cup

In a medium-sized heavy saucepan, melt the butter over moderate heat. When the foam subsides, add the onion and garlic. Cook, stirring occasionally, for 8-10 minutes, or until the onion is soft and golden.

Pour in the stock. Add the lemon juice, parsley, bay leaf and peas.

Bring the soup to the boil, stirring constantly. Reduce the heat to low, cover the pan and simmer the soup, stirring occasionally, for 30 minutes.

Remove the pan from the heat. Remove and discard the bay leaf. Put the contents of the pan through a food mill into a medium-sized bowl. Rinse the pan and pour the soup back into it.

Return the pan to moderate heat and stir in the ham. Cook, stirring occasionally, for 10 minutes.

To freeze: Cool. Pour into a rigid container leaving 1cm (½ inch) headspace. Seal, label and freeze.

To serve: Reheat frozen soup over low heat, stirring frequently. Stir in the cream and cook for 3 minutes. Do not allow the soup to boil.

Remove the pan from the heat and turn the soup into a warmed soup tureen. Serve immediately with crusty bread and butter.

Roman Aubergine [Eggplant]   Ⓛ Ⓛ

Above: Roman Aubergine [Eggplant] is a different way to serve aubergine [eggplant].

6-8 SERVINGS	Metric/UK/	US
Butter	40g/1½oz	3 tbsp
Butter, melted	1 teaspoon	1 tsp
Dry breadcrumbs	40g/1½oz	½ cup
Large aubergine [eggplant], peeled, cut into 1cm [½ inch] thick slices	1/1	1
Salt	1 teaspoon	1 tsp
Dried oregano	1 teaspoon	1 tsp
Parmesan cheese, grated	50g/2oz	½ cup
TOMATO SAUCE		
Olive oil	2 tablespoons	2 tbsp
Frozen onion, finely chopped	75g/3oz	3oz
Garlic clove, crushed	1/1	1
Canned peeled tomatoes	400g/14oz	14oz
Salt	1 teaspoon	1 tsp
Black pepper	½ teaspoon	½ tsp
Dried basil	1 teaspoon	1 tsp
Dried oregano	1 teaspoon	1 tsp

Preheat the oven to very hot 230°C (Gas Mark 8, 450°F). With the teaspoon of butter, grease a large baking sheet. Set aside.

To make the tomato sauce, in a medium-sized saucepan, heat the oil over moderate heat. When the oil is hot, add the onion and garlic. Cook, stirring occasionally, for 5-7 minutes or until the onion is soft and translucent but not brown. Add the tomatoes with the can juice, the salt, pepper, basil and oregano. Stir well. Reduce the heat to moderately low and simmer the sauce, stirring occasionally, for 25-30 minutes or until it is very thick.

Meanwhile, place the remaining melted butter in a shallow dish and the breadcrumbs on a sheet of greaseproof or waxed paper. Dip each aubergine [eggplant] slice first in the butter and then in the breadcrumbs, coating them on both sides. Place the slices on the baking sheet and sprinkle over the salt.

Place the baking sheet in the oven and bake the aubergine [eggplant] slices for 20 minutes or until they are tender and lightly browned.

Remove the baking sheet from the oven. Top each aubergine [eggplant] slice with a spoonful of the tomato sauce. Sprinkle over the oregano and Parmesan cheese.

To freeze: Cool. Freeze free-flow. When firm pack the aubergines into a rigid container. Seal and label.

To serve: Preheat the oven to 180°C (Gas Mark 4, 350°F). Place the frozen aubergines on a baking sheet and bake in the oven for 15-20 minutes or until the topping is lightly browned. Remove the baking sheet from the oven and serve the Roman Augergines [Eggplants] immediately.

Chili con Carne

Ⓛ Ⓛ Ⓛ

6 SERVINGS	Metric/UK/	US
Olive oil	2 tablespoons	2 tbsp
Frozen onions, finely sliced	225g/8oz	8oz
Garlic cloves, chopped	2/2	2
Lean minced [ground] beef, thawed	675g/1½lb	1½lb
Canned tomatoes	225g/8oz	8oz
Canned tomato purée	75g/3oz	3oz
Bay leaf	1/1	1
Ground cumin	1 teaspoon	1 tsp
Dried oregano	1 teaspoon	1 tsp
Cayenne pepper	1 teaspoon	1 tsp
Mild chilli powder	2 tablespoons	2 tbsp
Salt	2 teaspoons	2 tsp
Beef stock	350ml/12fl oz	1½ cups
Canned red kidney beans, drained	400g/14oz	14oz

In a large frying pan, heat the oil over moderate heat. Add the onions and garlic and fry them for 5-6 minutes, stirring constantly. Add the meat and brown it, stirring from time to time to make sure the meat breaks up properly and does not stick to the pan.

Put the mixture into a large, heavy saucepan and, mixing well, add the tomatoes, tomato purée, bay leaf, cumin, oregano, cayenne pepper, chilli powder, salt and stock. Cover the pan and bring the liquids to the boil over moderate heat. Reduce the heat to low and simmer the mixture, stirring occasionally, for 1 hour. Add the kidney beans.

To freeze: Cool. Pour into a rigid container. Seal, label and freeze.

To serve: Reheat Chili con Carne over a low heat, stirring frequently. When completely thawed simmer for a further 30 minutes. Remove the bay leaf and serve with chilled lager.

Below: Chili con Carne.

Parsley and Fish Pie

Ⓛ Ⓛ

4 SERVINGS	Metric/UK/	US
Milk	300ml/10fl oz	1¼ cups
Frozen onion, sliced	25g/1oz	1oz
Dried marjoram	½ teaspoon	½ tsp
Dried dill	¼ teaspoon	¼ tsp
Bay leaf	1/1	1
Salt	¾ teaspoon	¾ tsp
Black pepper	½ teaspoon	½ tsp
Butter	25g/1oz	2 tbsp
Flour	25g/1oz	¼ cup
Frozen white fish, cooked, skinned and flaked	450g/1lb	1lb
Chopped fresh parsley	8 tablespoons	8 tbsp
Lemon juice	1 teaspoon	1 tsp
Puff pastry, thawed	675g/1½lb	1½lb
Egg yolk	1/1	1
Milk	2 tablespoons	2 tbsp

Place the milk, frozen onion, marjoram, dill, bay leaf, salt and pepper in a medium-sized saucepan. Set the pan over moderately low heat and infuse the milk for 10 minutes.

Remove the pan from the heat and strain the milk into a small mixing bowl. Discard the contents of the strainer.

In a medium-sized saucepan, melt the butter over moderate heat. Remove the pan from the heat and, with a wooden spoon, stir in the flour to make a smooth paste. Gradually add the strained milk, stirring constantly. Return the pan to the heat and cook, stirring constantly, for 2-3 minutes or until the sauce is very thick and smooth.

Remove the pan from the heat. Stir in the fish, parsley and lemon juice and set aside.

On a lightly floured surface, roll the puff pastry out into a large square approximately ½cm (¼ inch) thick. With a sharp knife, trim the edges of the pastry to straighten them. Moisten the edges with a little cold water. With the rolling pin, lift the pastry on to a large baking sheet. Spoon the fish filling on to the centre of the pastry. Lift each of the four corners of the pastry up and over the filling until they meet in the centre. Pinch the points of the corners together to seal them.

Using a pastry brush, coat the dough with the egg yolk beaten with the 2 tablespoons of milk.

To freeze: Freeze free-flow. When firm close wrap the pie in foil and place in a polythene [plastic] bag. Seal and label.

To serve: Preheat the oven to 180°C (Gas Mark 4, 350°F). Place frozen pie on a baking sheet and bake in the oven for 40-50 minutes or until the pastry is golden brown.

Remove the baking sheet from the oven. Using two spatulas or fish slices, transfer the pie to a warmed serving dish and serve at once.

Dijon Kidneys   Ⓛ Ⓛ

4 SERVINGS	Metric/UK/	US
Lambs' or sheeps' kidneys, thawed	575g/1¼lb	1¼lb
Butter or margarine	1 tablespoon	1 tbsp
Cooking oil	1 tablespoon	1 tbsp
Flour	2 tablespoons	2 tbsp
Milk	300ml/10fl oz	1¼ cups
French mustard	2-3 tablespoons	2-3 tbsp
Salt		
Freshly ground black pepper		
Coarsely chopped parsley	6 tablespoons	6 tbsp

Clean, skin and core the kidneys carefully. Cut them into large pieces.

Heat the butter and oil in a large thick-bottomed saucepan. Place the kidneys in the pan and cook over medium heat for 4-5 minutes, turning them constantly to ensure even cooking.

Using a perforated spoon lift the kidneys from the pan on to a dish and set aside.

Add the flour to the fat remaining in pan. When it is well-amalgamated pour on the milk and stir over medium heat until a smooth thick sauce is obtained.

Stir in the mustard, season to taste with salt and pepper and add the chopped parsley. Simmer gently for 5 minutes.

Put the kidneys and their juices back into the pan and stir them into the sauce.

To freeze: Cool. Pour into a rigid container. Seal, label and freeze.

To serve: Reheat the frozen kidneys over a gentle heat, stirring frequently.

Turn the contents of the pan into the centre of a serving dish. Surround with a ring of plain boiled rice and serve immediately.

Left: Fish in a creamy sauce flavoured with parsley and enveloped in a light puff pastry, Parsley and Fish Pie makes an excellent supper dish for the family.

Below: Mustard and parsley sauce makes Dijon Kidneys popular even with those who claim to dislike kidneys.

onions are beginning to brown. Stir in the tomatoes with their can juice and cook the mixture for a further 3-4 minutes.

Return the meat to the casserole and add the groundnuts, stock, salt, pepper, cayenne and marjoram.

Bring the liquid to the boil and reduce the heat to low. Cover the casserole and simmer for 1½ hours.

To freeze: Remove the stew from the casserole. Wash the casserole and line with foil, leaving enough to cover the top. Replace the stew and fold the extra foil over the top of the casserole. Freeze. When frozen remove the foil parcel and place in a polythene [plastic] bag. Seal and label.

To serve: Preheat the oven to 180°C (Gas Mark 4, 350°F). Unwrap the foil parcel and replace frozen stew in the casserole. Cook in the oven for 1 hour or until the meat is tender when pierced with the point of a sharp knife. Remove the casserole from the oven and serve with plain boiled rice and fried bananas.

Two unusual dishes, (left) Groundnut Stew from West Africa and (right) Pastitsio from Greece.

Pastitsio   ⓁⓁ

4-6 SERVINGS	Metric/UK/	US
Oil or dripping	2 tablespoons	2 tbsp
Frozen onions, finely chopped	175g/6oz	6oz
Minced [ground] beef or lamb, thawed	450g/1lb	1lb
Canned tomato concentrate	40g/1½oz	1½oz
Salt		
Freshly ground black pepper		
Garlic clove, crushed	1/1	1
A pinch of cinnamon		
A pinch of dried thyme		
Rigatoni [long macaroni]	225g/8oz	8oz
Butter or margarine	25g/1oz	2 tbsp
Flour	25g/1oz	¼ cup
Milk	400ml/15fl oz	2 cups
Freshly grated nutmeg		
Grated cheese	75g/3oz	¾ cup
Natural yogurt	150ml/5fl oz	⅝ cup

Warm the oil or dripping in a large frying pan and fry the onions until they start to brown.

Add the meat and tomato concentrate and stir well with a fork to prevent lumps from forming. Sprinkle on the seasonings and cook for a few minutes adding a little beef stock if the mixture is too dry.

Cook the rigatoni in plenty of salted boiling water in an uncovered pan, then drain thoroughly.

Meanwhile prepare a white sauce with the margarine, flour and milk. Season generously with salt, pepper, nutmeg and half the grated cheese. Remove the pan from the heat and stir in the yogurt.

Line a large greased flameproof dish with the thoroughly drained pasta, spoon a third of the sauce over the top and cover with the meat mixture. Pour on the remaining sauce and sprinkle the rest of the cheese on top.

To freeze: Cool. Cover the top of the dish with foil and place it in a polythene [plastic] bag. Seal, label and freeze.

To serve: Preheat the oven 180°C (Gas Mark 4, 350°F). Remove the foil cover and cook the frozen Pastitsio in the oven for about 1 hour or until the cheese is golden brown. Serve with a green salad.

Groundnut Stew   ⓁⓁⓁ

4-6 SERVINGS	Metric/UK/	US
Vegetable oil	4 tablespoons	4 tbsp
Cubed stewing steak, thawed	900g/2lb	2lb
Frozen onions, thinly sliced	350g/12oz	12oz
Diced frozen green peppers	225g/8oz	8oz
Canned peeled tomatoes	400g/14oz	14oz
Groundnuts, shelled, roasted and skinned	175g/6oz	6oz
Beef stock	1.20ltr/2pts	5 cups
Salt	1½ teaspoons	1½ tsp
Black pepper	½ teaspoon	½ tsp
Cayenne pepper	¼ teaspoon	¼ tsp
Dried marjoram	1 teaspoon	1 tsp

In a large, heavy flameproof casserole, heat the oil over moderate heat. When the oil is hot, add the meat cubes and cook them, turning occasionally, for 5-8 minutes, or until the meat is evenly browned on all sides.

With a slotted spoon, transfer the meat from the casserole to a plate and set aside.

Add the onions and green peppers to the casserole and fry them, stirring occasionally, for 6-8 minutes, or until the

Berry Torte

Ⓛ Ⓛ

6 SERVINGS	Metric/UK/	US
Butter	75g/3oz	⅜ cup
Butter, melted	1 teaspoon	1 tsp
Digestive biscuits [graham crackers], **crushed**	175g/6oz	3 cups
Sugar	225g/8oz	1 cup
Full fat cream cheese	675g/1½lb	1½lb
Eggs	4/4	4
Lemon juice	1 teaspoon	1 tsp
Cornflour [cornstarch],	2 teaspoons	2 tsp
Grated lemon rind	2 teaspoons	2 tsp
Frozen blackcurrants	350g/12oz	12oz
Water	3 tablespoons	3 tbsp

Preheat the oven to moderate 180°C (Gas Mark 4, 350°F). Grease a 20cm (8 inch) round cake tin with a removable bottom with 1 teaspoon of butter.

In a medium-sized mixing bowl, combine the crushed biscuits [crackers], 85g (3 oz) [⅜ cup] sugar and the melted butter with a wooden spoon. Lightly press the crumbs into the buttered tin, covering the bottom and halfway up the sides of the pan evenly.

In a medium-sized mixing bowl, beat the cream cheese with a wooden spoon or a fork until it is smooth. Gradually beat the remaining sugar, eggs, lemon juice and half the lemon rind into the cheese, until it is a thick, smooth cream.

Pour the cream cheese mixture into the lined cake tin. Bake in the oven for 35 minutes. Leave the torte to cool and then chill it in the refrigerator overnight.

In a medium-sized mixing bowl, combine the cornflour [cornstarch] with the water and mix in the berries and remaining lemon rind. Pour the mixture into a saucepan and cook for 2-3 minutes over moderate heat stirring once or twice. Remove the mixture from the heat and leave to cool.

Spread the berry mixture evenly over the torte.

To freeze: Freeze free-flow. Carefully place the torte in a rigid container, avoid damaging the shape of the torte. Seal and label.

To serve: Thaw in the refrigerator for 6-8 hours.

Below left: Berry Torte.
Below right: Pumpkin Pie is even
more economical to make when
pumpkin is in season.
Right:
Whipped Raspberry Pudding.

48

Pumpkin Pie Ⓛ Ⓛ

6 SERVINGS	Metric/UK/	US
Flan case made with shortcrust pastry, uncooked	1x23cm/1x9inch	
Brown sugar	125g/4oz	⅔ cup
Salt	⅛ teaspoon	⅛ tsp
Ground cinnamon	1½ teaspoons	1½ tsp
Ground ginger	½ teaspoon	½ tsp
Ground cloves	¼ teaspoon	¼ tsp
Canned puréed pumpkin	700g/24oz	24oz
Eggs, lightly beaten	3/3	3
Single cream [light cream]	300ml/10fl oz	1¼ cups

Place the flan case on a baking sheet.

Preheat the oven to fairly hot 190°C (Gas Mark 5, 375°F).

Combine the sugar, salt, cinnamon, ginger and cloves in a small mixing bowl. Place the pumpkin purée in a large mixing bowl, add the eggs, and mix well with a wooden spoon. With the spoon, gradually stir the sugar and spice mixture and the cream into the pumpkin mixture and beat well until it is smooth.

Pour the pumpkin mixture into the flan case. Place the baking sheet in the oven. Bake the pie for 45-50 minutes or until a knife inserted in the filling comes out clean. Remove the baking sheet from the oven.

To freeze: Cool. Freeze free-flow. Carefully place the pie in a rigid container, avoid damaging the shape of the pie. Seal and label.

To serve: Thaw in the refrigerator for 6-8 hours.

Whipped Raspberry Pudding Ⓛ Ⓛ

6 SERVINGS	Metric/UK/	US
Frozen raspberries, thawed	675g/1½lb	1½lb
Castor [superfine] sugar	125g/4oz	½ cup
Semolina	50g/2oz	½ cup
Almond essence [extract]	⅛ teaspoon	⅛ tsp

Pour the raspberries into a medium-sized fine wire strainer held over a medium-sized mixing bowl. Using the back of a wooden spoon, rub the fruit through the strainer to form a purée. Discard the pips [seeds] in the strainer. Alternatively, blend the fruit in an electric blender.

Pour the puréed fruit into a medium-sized saucepan and bring to the boil over moderate heat. Gradually add the sugar and the semolina, stirring constantly. Reduce the heat to low and simmer the mixture for 10 minutes, stirring occasionally.

Remove the pan from the heat and transfer the mixture to a large mixing bowl. Stir in the almond essence [extract]. Using a wire whisk or rotary beater, beat the mixture for 15 minutes or until it has doubled in volume and is light and fluffy.

To freeze: Pour the mixture into a rigid container. Seal, label and freeze.

To serve: Thaw the pudding in the refrigerator for 6-8 hours, then spoon the pudding into 6 individual serving dishes and serve immediately with chilled whipped cream.

Kid's grub

Mushroom Rolls ⓁⓁ

20 ROLLS	Metric/UK/	US
Butter	150g/5oz	$\frac{5}{8}$ cup
Frozen onion, chopped	125g/4oz	4oz
Frozen mushrooms, chopped	225g/8oz	8oz
Black pepper	$\frac{1}{4}$ teaspoon	$\frac{1}{4}$ tsp
Fresh lemon juice	1 tablespoon	1 tbsp
Fresh breadcrumbs	50g/2oz	1 cup
Chicken stock	50ml/2fl oz	$\frac{1}{4}$ cup
Finely chopped fresh parsley	1 tablespoon	1 tbsp
Lean bacon slices, thawed and rinds removed	20/20	20

In a large saucepan, melt 113g (4oz) [$\frac{1}{2}$ cup] of the butter over low heat. When the foam subsides, add the onion and mushrooms. Gently simmer, stirring occasionally, for 5 minutes or until the mushrooms are soft. Remove the pan from the heat.

Using a slotted spoon, transfer the mushrooms and onion to a large mixing bowl. Soak the breadcrumbs in the stock. Add the pepper, lemon juice, breadcrumb mixture and parsley. With a potato masher or fork, mash the ingredients together until they form a paste.

Lay the bacon slices out flat. Spread each slice with a little of the paste. Roll up the bacon slices and secure each roll with cocktail stick.

In a small saucepan, melt the remaining butter over moderate heat. Remove the pan from the heat and brush the melted butter over the rolls.

To freeze: Cool. Freeze free-flow. When firm pack rolls into rigid containers. Seal and label.

To serve: Place the rolls under a moderate grill [broiler] and grill [broil], turning frequently, for about 10-15 minutes, or until the bacon is crisp. Remove the cocktail sticks and serve at once.

Bloater Paste ⓁⓁⓁ

340g [12oz] PASTE	Metric/UK/	US
Fresh white breadcrumbs	125g/4oz	2 cups
Water	175ml/6fl oz	$\frac{3}{4}$ cup
Bloaters, cooked, skinned, filleted and flaked	4/4	4
Butter, melted	50g/2oz	$\frac{1}{4}$ cup
Juice of $\frac{1}{2}$ lemon		
Black pepper	$\frac{1}{2}$ teaspoon	$\frac{1}{2}$ tsp
Cayenne pepper	$\frac{1}{2}$ teaspoon	$\frac{1}{2}$ tsp

Place the breadcrumbs in a mixing bowl and pour over the water. When the breadcrumbs are thoroughly soaked, squeeze out all the excess water.

Place the breadcrumbs, bloaters, butter, lemon juice, pepper and cayenne in a mortar and pound them with a pestle until they form a smooth paste. Alternatively, blend all the ingredients in an electric blender until the paste is smooth.

To freeze: Spoon the paste into small containers. Seal, label and freeze.

To serve: Thaw for 12 hours in the refrigerator and serve on thickly buttered toast.

Hamburgers ⓁⓁⓁ

6 SERVINGS	Metric/UK/	US
Lean minced [ground] beef, thawed	1.35kg/3lb	3lb
Fresh breadcrumbs	50g/2oz	1 cup
Salt	1 teaspoon	1 tsp
Black pepper	$\frac{1}{2}$ teaspoon	$\frac{1}{2}$ tsp
Dried thyme	$\frac{1}{2}$ teaspoon	$\frac{1}{2}$ tsp
Egg, lightly beaten	1/1	1
ACCOMPANIMENTS		
Medium-sized tomatoes, thinly sliced	3/3	3
Large onion, thinly sliced and pushed out into rings	1/1	1
Large lettuce leaves	6/6	6
Hamburger or large soft buns	6/6	6
Butter	50g/2oz	$\frac{1}{4}$ cup

Bean Rarebit

LLL

4 SERVINGS	Metric/UK/	US
Butter	25g/1oz	2 tbsp
Frozen onion, finely chopped	125g/4oz	4oz
Frozen, diced green pepper, finely chopped	125g/4oz	4oz
Canned kidney beans, drained	400g/14oz	14oz
Canned baked beans	400g/14oz	14oz
Tomato ketchup	4 tablespoons	4 tbsp
Worcestershire sauce	1 tablespoon	1 tbsp
Salt	$\frac{1}{2}$ teaspoon	$\frac{1}{2}$ tsp
Black pepper	1 teaspoon	1 tsp
Mild chilli powder	1 teaspoon	1 tsp
Cheddar cheese, grated	175g/6oz	$1\frac{1}{2}$ cups

In a medium-sized frying pan, melt the butter over moderate heat. When the foam subsides, add the onion and green pepper and fry, stirring occasionally, for 5-7 minutes or until the onion is soft and translucent but not brown. Stir in the kidney beans, baked beans with the can juice, ketchup, Worcestershire sauce, salt, pepper and chilli powder and stir well to mix. Cook the mixture, stirring occasionally, for a further 5 minutes. Stir in the cheese.

To freeze: Cool. Pour the mixture into a rigid container. Seal, label and freeze.

To serve: Place the frozen mixture in a pan and thaw over a low heat, stirring frequently until the mixture is hot and thick.

Remove the pan from the heat. Place 4 large slices of hot buttered toast on individual serving plates and spoon the bean mixture over them. Serve at once.

Below: Bean Rarebit. Left: A Hamburger is a quick and popular meal for children.

In a medium-sized mixing bowl, combine the beef, breadcrumbs, salt, pepper, thyme and egg, using your hands to mix the ingredients together thoroughly.

Form the beef mixture into six balls and flatten them into patty shapes.

To freeze: Freeze free-flow. When firm stack together and wrap all six hamburgers in foil. Place the package in a polythene [plastic] bag. Seal and label.

To serve: Separate the hamburgers and place under a hot grill [broiler] for 3-4 minutes on each side, or until hamburgers are well browned. Then reduce the temperature to moderate and grill [broil] for a further 5-7 minutes on each side, or until the hamburgers are well cooked.

When the hamburgers are cooked, place one on each bun and transfer them to six individual serving plates. Serve immediately, with the accompaniments, and a selection of pickles and relishes, tomato ketchup, mayonnaise, mustard, potato crisps [chips] or French-fried potatoes.

Cheese and Sardine Fritters ⓁⓁⓁ

4 SERVINGS	Metric/UK	US
Fresh sardines, cleaned	900g/2lb	2lb
Cheddar cheese, grated	275g/10oz	2½ cups
Eggs, lightly beaten	2/2	2
Juice of 1 lemon		
Flour	175g/6oz	1½ cups
Freshly ground black pepper	½ teaspoon	½ tsp
Fine dry breadcrumbs	50g/2oz	⅔ cup
Sufficient vegetable oil for deep-frying		
GARNISH		
Lemon slices		

Preheat the grill [broiler] to high.

Wash the sardines under cold running water and pat them dry with kitchen paper towels.

Place the sardines on the rack in the grill [broiler] pan and place the pan under the grill [broiler]. Grill [broil] for 6 minutes, turning the fish occasionally. Remove the grill [broiler] pan from the heat.

Place the sardines on a flat surface. Remove and discard the head, tail and spine from each sardine. Place the flesh in a medium-sized mixing bowl. Add the cheese, 1 egg and the lemon juice. Using a wooden spoon, blend the mixture well.

On a plate combine the flour, pepper and the breadcrumbs. Place the remaining egg on a second plate.

Roll the sardine mixture into small patties and dip each patty first in the beaten egg, then in the flour mixture, shaking off any excess.

Fill a large deep-frying pan one-third full with vegetable oil. Set the pan over moderate heat and heat the oil until it registers 190°C (375°F) on a deep-fat thermometer or until a small cube of stale bread dropped into the oil turns golden brown in 40 seconds. Place the patties, a few at a time, in a deep-frying basket and lower the basket into the oil. Fry the patties for 2-5 minutes. Drain well.

To freeze: Freeze free-flow. When firm pack the fritters into a polythene [plastic] bag. Seal and label.

To serve: Fry the frozen fritters in hot fat for 2-3 minutes until golden brown. Remove the basket from the oil and transfer the fritters to kitchen paper towels to drain. Keep warm while you fry and drain the remaining patties in the same way.

Place the fritters on a heated serving dish, garnish with the lemon slices and serve immediately.

Lamb Hotpot ⓁⓁⓁ

4-6 SERVINGS	Metric/UK/	US
Vegetable oil	1 tablespoon	1 tbsp
Butter	25g/1oz	2 tbsp
Loin of lamb, thawed, chined and trimmed of excess fat	1.75kg/1x4lb	1x4lb
Frozen onion, thinly sliced	175g/6oz	6oz
Large potatoes, peeled and sliced	4/4	4
Canned peeled tomatoes, coarsely chopped	400g/14oz	14oz
Salt	1 teaspoon	1 tsp
Black pepper	½ teaspoon	½ tsp
Dried thyme	1 teaspoon	1 tsp

In a large, heavy flameproof casserole, heat the oil and butter over moderate heat. When the foam subsides, add the lamb and cook, turning the meat occasionally with tongs, for 8-10 minutes, or until it is lightly browned on all sides.

Using two large forks, lift the meat out of the casserole and set it aside.

Add the onion to the casserole and fry, stirring occasionally, for 5 minutes. Add the potatoes and fry, stirring occasionally, for 5-6 minutes, or until they are lightly browned.

Stir in the tomatoes with the can juice, the salt, pepper and thyme. Cook the mixture, stirring constantly, for 2-3 minutes, or until it is hot but not boiling. Reduce the heat to low, add the lamb and cover the casserole. Braise for 1 hour or until the meat is tender when pierced with a sharp knife.

Remove the casserole from the heat. Using two large forks, lift the meat out of the casserole and transfer it to a carving board.

With a sharp knife, separate the meat into chops and place the chops to one side, together with the potatoes.

Return the casserole to moderate heat and boil the sauce, stirring constantly, for 3-4 minutes, or until it has reduced slightly. Replace the meat and potatoes.

To freeze: Remove the hotpot from the casserole. Wash the casserole and line with foil, leaving enough to cover the top. Replace the hotpot and fold the extra foil over the top of the casserole. Freeze. When frozen remove the foil parcel from the casserole and place in a polythene [plastic] bag. Seal and label.

To serve: Preheat the oven to 180°C (Gas Mark 4, 350°F). Unwrap the foil parcel and replace frozen hotpot in the casserole. Cook in the oven for 40-50 minutes. Serve with peas.

Maple Sparerib Casserole ⓁⓁ

4 SERVINGS	Metric/UK/	US
Maple syrup	150ml/5fl oz	⅝ cup
Cayenne pepper	¼ teaspoon	¼ tsp
Salt	1 teaspoon	1 tsp
Black pepper	½ teaspoon	½ tsp
Garlic cloves, crushed	1/1	1
Tomato purée	2 tablespoons	2 tbsp
Prepared French or German mustard	1 tablespoon	1 tbsp
Lemon juice	2 tablespoons	2 tbsp
Spareribs of pork, thawed, trimmed of excess fat and cut into 2-rib serving pieces	1.75kg/4lb	4lb

Preheat the oven to fairly hot 200°C (Gas Mark 6, 400°F).

In a small mixing bowl, combine the syrup, cayenne, salt, pepper, garlic, tomato purée and mustard. Stir in the lemon juice. Set the mixture aside.

Put the spareribs in a large roasting tin. Place the tin in the upper part of the oven. Roast for 30 minutes.

Remove the tin from the oven. Using tongs, remove the spareribs and set them aside on a dish. Pour away the fat that has accumulated in the tin.

To freeze: Cool the spareribs and place in a rigid container. Pour over the maple syrup mixture. Seal, label and freeze.

To serve: Thaw the sparerib casserole in the refrigerator for 12 hours. Preheat the oven to 180°C (Gas Mark 4, 350°F). Transfer the sparerib casserole to a roasting tin and roast in the oven for 45 minutes, basting frequently, or until the ribs are brown and glazed.

Remove the tin from the oven. Transfer the spareribs to a heated dish and serve immediately with a green salad.

Above: Children will love eating Maple Sparerib Casserole with their fingers.
Below: Tasty Lamb Hotpot.

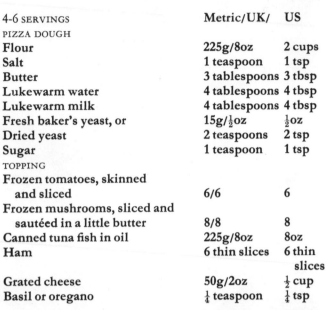

Pizza Quattro Stagioni

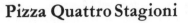

4-6 SERVINGS	Metric/UK/	US
PIZZA DOUGH		
Flour	225g/8oz	2 cups
Salt	1 teaspoon	1 tsp
Butter	3 tablespoons	3 tbsp
Lukewarm water	4 tablespoons	4 tbsp
Lukewarm milk	4 tablespoons	4 tbsp
Fresh baker's yeast, or	15g/½oz	½oz
Dried yeast	2 teaspoons	2 tsp
Sugar	1 teaspoon	1 tsp
TOPPING		
Frozen tomatoes, skinned and sliced	6/6	6
Frozen mushrooms, sliced and sautéed in a little butter	8/8	8
Canned tuna fish in oil	225g/8oz	8oz
Ham	6 thin slices	6 thin slices
Grated cheese	50g/2oz	½ cup
Basil or oregano	¼ teaspoon	¼ tsp

Sift the flour and salt into a warmed bowl. Rub the butter into the flour. Cream the yeast and sugar together and add to the lukewarm liquids. (If you use dried yeast, dissolve the sugar in the water and sprinkle the yeast on the top. Leave for 5 minutes until it begins to bubble then add the milk to it.)

Above: The four different toppings of Pizza Quattro Stagioni make an exciting pizza.

54

Add the yeast mixture to the flour and beat thoroughly. Cover and leave to rise in a warm place until double its bulk: this will take about 40 minutes.

Flour the dough and pat into a round on a floured baking sheet, and cover with the skinned and sliced tomatoes, the sliced and sautéed mushrooms, flakes of tuna fish, and the thin slices of ham. Sprinkle grated cheese and a little basil or oregano over the top.

To freeze: Freeze free-flow. When firm loosely wrap in foil. Place in a polythene [plastic] bag. Seal and label.

To serve: Preheat the oven to 200°C (Gas Mark 6, 400°F). Place the frozen pizza on a baking sheet and moisten the top of the pizza with a little oil. Bake at the top of the oven for 30-35 minutes.

Ohio Meat Pie

6 SERVINGS	Metric/UK/	US
Vegetable oil	3 tablespoons	3 tbsp
Frozen onions, sliced	225g/8oz	8oz
Lean minced [ground] beef,		
thawed	900g/2lb	2lb
Frozen carrots, diced	350g/12oz	12oz
Frozen green pepper, diced	125g/4oz	4oz
Frozen courgettes [zucchini],		
sliced	450g/1lb	1lb
Raisins	50g/2oz	⅓ cup
Salt	1½ teaspoons	1½ tsp
Pepper	½ teaspoon	½ tsp
Canned baked beans	425g/15oz	15oz
Canned sweetcorn, drained	350g/12oz	12oz
Butter	75g/3oz	⅜ cup
Flour	75g/3oz	¾ cup
Milk	900ml/1½pts	3¾ cups
Cheddar cheese, grated	125g/4oz	1 cup
Egg yolks	4/4	4

In a large, deep frying pan, heat the oil over moderate heat. When the oil is hot add the onions and fry, stirring occasionally, for 8-10 minutes or until the onions are golden brown.

Add the meat and fry, stirring frequently, for 10 minutes or until the meat is well browned. Add the carrots, green pepper, courgettes [zucchini], raisins, 1 teaspoon of the salt and the pepper. Cover the pan, reduce the heat to low and simmer for 20-25 minutes or until the vegetables are tender.

Stir in the beans and corn and simmer, uncovered, for a further 2 minutes.

Remove the pan from the heat and spoon the mixture into a large baking dish. Set aside.

In a medium-sized saucepan, melt the butter over moderate heat. Remove the pan from the heat and, with a wooden spoon, stir in the flour to make a smooth paste. Gradually add the milk, stirring constantly. When all the milk has been added, return the pan to the heat. Cook the sauce for 3-4 minutes, stirring constantly, until it comes to the boil and is thick and smooth. Stir in the cheese and the remaining salt. Remove the pan from the heat.

In a small mixing bowl, beat the egg yolks with a fork until they are well mixed. Add 4-5 tablespoons of the hot sauce. Stir the egg yolk mixture into the sauce.

Pour the sauce over the meat mixture in the baking dish.

To freeze: Cool. Cover the baking dish with foil and place in a polythene [plastic] bag. Seal, label and freeze.

To serve: Thaw the meat pie in the refrigerator for 12 hours. Preheat the oven to 180°C (Gas Mark 4, 350°F). Remove the foil and place the dish at the top of the oven and bake for 25-30 minutes, or until the top is lightly browned. Remove the dish from the oven and serve immediately from the dish.

Left: An economical and unusual dish, Ohio Meat Pie can be made with any vegetables.

Teddy Bear Cake

Ⓛ

8 SERVINGS	Metric/UK/	US
Bought chocolate Swiss [jelly] rolls	4x8cm/4x3inch	
Buttercream icing, chocolate-flavoured	450g/1lb	1lb
Swiss [jelly] roll with cream filling	1x23cm/1x9inch	
Coloured sweets [candies]	12/12	12

Using a sharp knife, cut a 1cm (½inch) slice off the ends of two of the small Swiss [jelly] rolls. Cut one of the slices in half, leave the other slice whole and set them aside.

Spread 1 teaspoon of the buttercream icing over one end of the large Swiss [jelly] roll and stand it upright, iced end down, on a cake board. This will form the body and head of the bear. Spread ½ teaspoon of the buttercream icing along one end and one side of each of the four small Swiss [jelly] rolls. Arrange the two slightly longer rolls so that the iced ends are attached to the base of the bear's body and the iced sides are flat against the cake board. These will form the bear's legs. Arrange the two smaller rolls so that the iced sides lie upright against the sides of the bear's body. These will form the bear's arms. Spread a little icing over one side of the whole reserved slice and place it in the centre of the bear's face to form its snout. Spread a little icing over the cut edges of the halved slice and place them, iced side down, on top of the large roll to form the bear's ears.

Using a flat-bladed knife, spread the remaining buttercream icing over the bear to completely cover it, roughing up the surface with the blade of the knife to give a fur-like appearance. Take care to mould the icing carefully to accentuate the bear-shape of the cake.

Use 9 of the sweets [candies] to form the nose, eyes and paws, and the remaining 3 sweets [candies] for buttons.

To freeze: Freeze free-flow. When firm pack very carefully in a large rigid container. Seal and label.

To serve: Thaw the cake in the refrigerator for 6-8 hours.

Mocha Ice-Cream Charlotte

Ⓛ

6-8 SERVINGS	Metric/UK/	US
Eggs, separated	4/4	4
Sifted icing [confectioners'] sugar	125g/4oz	1 cup
Coffee essence	4 tablespoons	4 tbsp
Double [heavy] cream, lightly whipped	300ml/½ pint	1¼ cups
DECORATION		
Plain [semi-sweet] chocolate finger biscuits [cookies]	450g/1lb	1lb

Whisk the egg whites until very stiff, then gradually whisk in the sugar. Beat the egg yolks with the coffee essence, then beat them gradually into the whisked whites. Carefully fold in the cream. Turn the mixture into a 20cm (8inch) cake tin; preferably one with a loose bottom.

To freeze: Cover lightly with foil and freeze. When firm place in a rigid container. Seal and label.

To serve: Allow the ice-cream to soften for 1 hour in the refrigerator. Turn the ice-cream out of the cake tin and press the chocolate biscuits [cookies] round the sides. If you have difficulty in making them stick to the ice-cream, run a hot knife quickly round the sides of the ice-cream to melt it. Tie the biscuits in place with a ribbon.

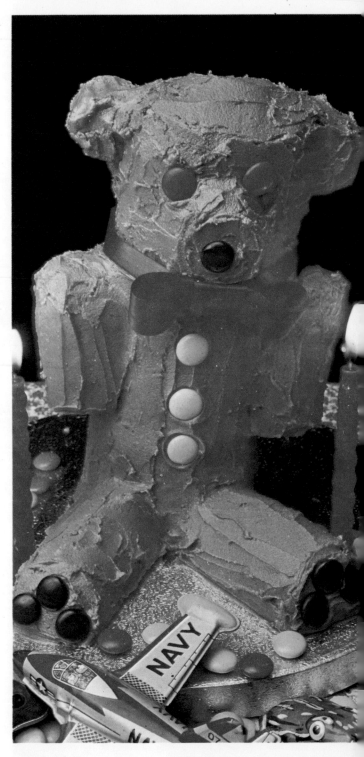

Above: This Teddy Bear Cake provides an imaginative centrepiece to any children's party. Simple to prepare and assemble from Swiss [Jelly] rolls.

Above right: Coriander Fruit Crumble will be particularly popular with children if you use the blackberries they have picked.
Right: Mocha Ice-Cream Charlotte is novel and attractive and sure to delight everyone.

Coriander Fruit Crumble ⓁⓁⓁ

4-6 SERVINGS	Metric/UK/	US
Butter or margarine	1 teaspoon	1 tsp
Frozen cooking [greening] apples, sliced	675g/1½lb	1½lb
Frozen blackberries	225g/8oz	8oz
Brown sugar	2 tablespoons	2 tbsp
Ground cinnamon	1 teaspoon	1 tsp
TOPPING		
Flour	125g/4oz	1 cup
Sugar	125g/4oz	½ cup
Butter or margarine	50g/2oz	¼ cup
Ground coriander	2 teaspoons	2 tsp

Grease a 2 litre (3 pint) [7½ cup] baking dish with the tea-spoon of butter or margarine.

Put the apples and blackberries in the baking dish and sprinkle them with the brown sugar and cinnamon. Set the baking dish aside.

To make the crumble topping, put the flour and sugar into a medium-sized mixing bowl. Add the butter or margarine and cut it into small pieces with a table knife. With your fingertips, rub the butter or margarine into the flour and sugar until the mixture resembles coarse breadcrumbs. Mix in the coriander.

Sprinkle the crumble topping over the fruit.

To freeze: Loosely wrap the dish in foil and place in a polythene [plastic] bag. Seal, label and freeze.

To serve: Preheat the oven to 180°C (Gas Mark 4, 350°F). Remove the foil and cook the crumble in the oven for 50-60 minutes. Remove the crumble from the oven and serve immediately, straight from the dish.

Ice-Cream Roll   Ⓛ Ⓛ

ONE ICE-CREAM ROLL	Metric/UK/	US
Vegetable oil	1 teaspoon	1 tsp
Eggs	3/3	3
Castor [superfine] sugar	75g/3oz	⅜ cup
Flour, sifted	75g/3oz	¾ cup
Vanilla essence [extract]	¼ teaspoon	¼ tsp
Sifted cornflour [cornstarch]	1 tablespoon	1 tbsp
FILLING		
Strawberry jam	125g/4oz	4oz
Vanilla ice-cream	16fl oz	2 cups

Preheat the oven to hot 220°C (Gas Mark 7, 425°F).

Line a 20 x 30cm (8 x 12 inch) Swiss [jelly] roll tin with non-stick silicone paper or aluminium foil. If you use foil, grease it with the oil. Set aside.

Put the eggs and sugar in a medium-sized heatproof mixing bowl. Place the bowl in a pan half-filled with hot water. Set the pan over low heat.

Using a wire whisk or rotary beater, beat the eggs and sugar together until the mixture is very thick and will make a ribbon trail on itself when the whisk is lifted. If an electric beater is used, no heat is required.

Remove the bowl from the saucepan. Using a metal spoon or spatula, fold in the flour and the vanilla essence [extract].

Pour the batter into the prepared tin and smooth it down with a flat-bladed knife.

Place the tin in the centre of the oven and bake for 8 minutes, or until a skewer inserted into the centre of the sponge comes out clean.

Below: Ice-Cream Roll made with bought ice-cream.

Remove the tin from the oven.

Lay a piece of greaseproof or waxed paper flat on the working surface and dust it with the cornflour [cornstarch]. Turn the sponge out on to the paper. Carefully remove the silicone paper or foil from the sponge.

With a sharp knife, make a shallow cut across the sponge about 6cm (2½inches) from the end, to make the rolling easier. With the help of the greaseproof or waxed paper, carefully roll up the sponge, Swiss [jelly] roll style, with the paper inside. Set the cake aside to cool completely.

When the cake is cold, carefully unroll it. Discard the greaseproof or waxed paper and, using a flat-bladed knife, spread the jam evenly over the surface of the cake. Spread the ice-cream thickly on top of the jam. Roll up the Swiss [jelly] roll.

To freeze: Freeze free-flow. When firm loosely wrap the roll in foil and place in a polythene [plastic] bag. Seal and label.

To serve: Thaw the roll in the refrigerator for 30 minutes or until the sponge is soft. Decorate with glacé cherries and angelica.

Gardening for freezing

If you grow some of your own fruit and vegetables, inevitably there comes a time when you have a surplus, and this is where a freezer is invaluable. By making sensible use of your garden you can save money, but if you are a beginner, do not set your sights too high. Do not try to grow enough produce for the whole year, this will result in a full time job, both in gardening and freezing. Choose the simplest varieties to grow and which freeze well. For example:—

Runner Beans
Broad [Lima] Beans
Carrots
Peas
Apples
Blackberries and Raspberries
Gooseberries
Rhubarb

Select 6 to 8 varieties of fruit or vegetable and aim for a 2¼ kg (5 lb) yield from each to freeze. The remainder of the harvest should be eaten fresh.

Vegetables to grow for your Freezer

VARIETIES	SOWING	HARVESTING
Beetroots [Beets] Boltardy, Detroit, Early Model, Golden Beet, Mono King Explorer, Ruby Queen, Snowhite. [U.S.: Early Wonder, Crosly's Egyptian.]	Sow from early April to mid-July. Plant seed 3 cm (1 inch) deep in rows 30 cm (12 inches) apart and space seed 10 cm (4 inches) apart. Thin out seedlings to 20 cm (8 inches).	Harvest from July to October when they are about the size of golf balls. Small tender young beetroots [beets] can be frozen whole. Larger beetroots [beets] should be sliced.
Beans, Broad [Lima] Dreadnought, Imperial Green Longpod, Imperial Green Windsor, Masterpiece.	Sow from April to May. Plant beans singly 3 cm (1 inch) deep in rows 75 cm (2.5 ft) apart and space beans 15 cm (6 inches) apart.	Harvest while the beans are still young, before a black eye has formed.
Beans, French [Snap] Brezo, Glamis, Limelight, Remus, Royalty, Tendergreen. [U.S.: Stringless Greenford, Bountiful, Pencil Pod Max.]	Sow from April to May. Plant seed 3 cm (1 inch) deep in rows 45 cm (18 inches) apart and space seed 15 cm (6 inches) apart.	Harvest from July to October while they are small enough to freeze whole.
Beans, Runner Blue Lake White Seeded, Crusader, Kelvedon Marvel, Kentucky Wonder, Romano, Violet Podded Stringless.	Sow from May and June. Plant seed 5 cm (2 inches) deep in double rows with 1.5 m (5 ft) between the rows and space seed 25 cm (10 inches) apart.	Harvest from July to October. Pick frequently and before the beans form inside the pods.
Broccoli Calabrese, Christmas Purple Sprouting, Early Purple Sprouting, Green Comet, Nine Star Perennial, White Sprouting.	Sow from March to May. Plant seed 1 cm ($\frac{1}{2}$ inch) deep and space seed 23 cm (9 inches) apart. Thin out seedlings to 15 cm (6 inches) as soon as large enough to handle. Transplant from May to June about 75 cm (2.5 ft) apart in both directions.	Harvest when the head is firm and the shoots are about 30 cm (12 inches) long.
Brussels Sprouts Achilles, British Allrounder, Citadel, Focus, Peer Gynt. [U.S.: Jade Cross Hybrid, Long Island Improved.]	Sow early summer. Plant seed 1 cm ($\frac{1}{2}$ inch) deep. Transplant when they have reached a height of 15 cm (6 inches). Allow 75 cm (2.5 ft) between both plants and rows.	Harvest from September to December as the sprouts form from the base of the stem. Only tiny button sprouts should be used for freezing.
Carrots Amsterdam Forcing, Champion Scarlet Horn, Chantenay, Cluseed New Model, Early Nantes. [U.S.: Goldinhart, Imperator.]	Sow from March to mid-July. Plant seed 1 cm ($\frac{1}{2}$ inch) deep in rows 30 cm (12 inches) apart. Thin out seedlings to 8 cm (3 inches) as soon as large enough to handle.	Harvest from June onwards when they are the size and shape of the middle finger and freeze whole. Larger carrots can be sliced.
Cauliflower Improved Snowball, Majestic. [U.S.: Snow King, Snow Crown, Purple Head.]	Sow under glass in late winter and thin out seedlings to 5 cm (2 inches) as soon as large enough to handle. Harden off in cold frames in March, but protect them from frost. Transplant to open ground as soon as possible, allowing 45 cm (18 inches) between rows and plants.	Harvest from June to September when the heads are small, compact and white. Freeze in florets.
Corn-on-the-cob Earliking, Early Extra Sweet, Honey and Cream, Honey Dew, John Innes, Northern Belle, Polar Vee. [U.S.: Golden Cross, Bantam, Iochief, Illini Xtra Sweet.]	Sow under glass in April. Plant seed 8 cm (3 inches) deep. Transplant in June in rows 90 cm (3 ft) apart and space seedlings 38 cm (15 inches) apart.	Harvest from August to September, when silk of the cob begins to turn a mustard colour.
Courgettes [Zucchinis] Early Gem. [U.S.: Fordhook, Golden Zucchini.]	Sow under glass in April, planting seeds singly 8 cm (3 inches) deep in peat pots or outdoors when safe from frost. Space the seedlings 30 cm (12 inches) apart.	Harvest from July to October when they are about 8 cm (3 inches) long. Courgettes can be frozen either whole or sliced.

Peas
Gloriosa, Hurst Green Shaft, Kelvedon Wonder, Little Marvel, Onward, Petit Pois Gullivert, Recette, Trio, Victory Freezer. [U.S.: Freezonian, Thomas Laxton, Nando, Alaska.]

Sow from March to June. Plant seed 5 cm (2 inches) deep in rows 20 cm (8 inches) apart and space seed 8 cm (3 inches) apart. The distance between rows should be as wide as the variety is tall. Supports should be provided as soon as the seed is sown.

Harvest from when the pods look full but there is still some give in them.

Spinach
Greenmarket, Perpetual. [U.S.: America, Bloomsdale Long Standing.]

Sow summer spinach from March to May and the winter variety from August to October. Plant seed 3 cm (1 inch) deep and in rows 30 cm (12 inches) apart. Thin out the seedlings to 8 cm (3 inches) apart.

Harvest when leaves are still young and bright in colour.

Tomatoes
Moneymaker, Potentate. [U.S.: Better Boy, Spring Giant Hybrid, Red Cherry, Yellow Plum, Sunray, Beefsteak, Oxheart.]

Sow indoors in a temperature of 16°C (60°F) in spring and prick off seedlings 8 cm (3 inches) apart. Move to an unheated greenhouse in summer or outside if the temperature does not fall below 10°C (50°F).

Harvest as they ripen. Tomatoes not ready by late autumn should be picked and ripened in a drawer in a warm room.

Above: Fresh or frozen baby carrots taste delicious on their own, but try adding a sprinkling of aniseed to the cooking water for an interesting combination of flavours.
Left: Although the brussels sprout is a member of the cabbage family, it does not produce a single head but a series of small compact sprouts in the joints of the leaves.

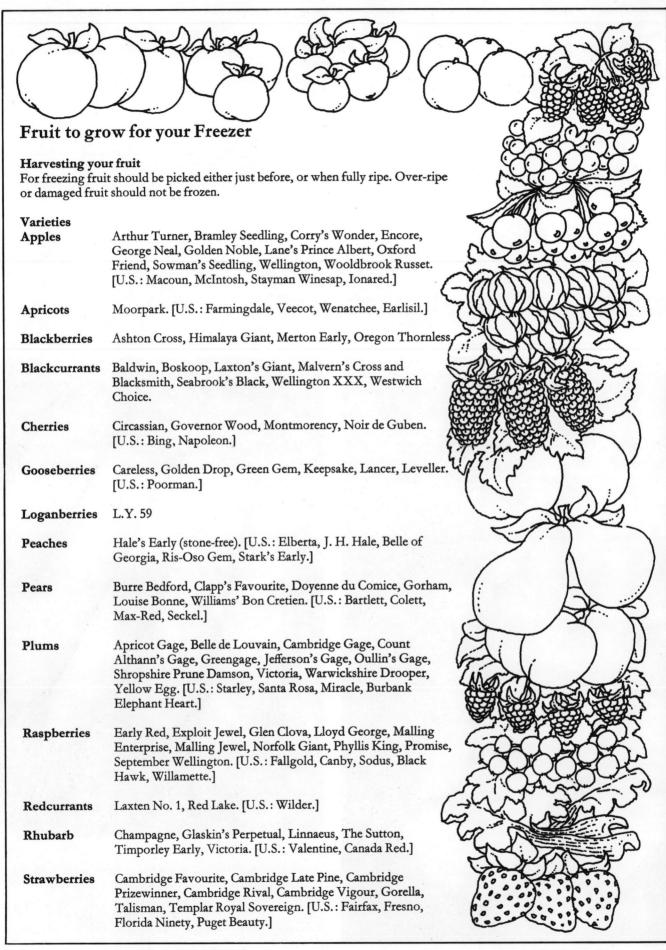

Fruit to grow for your Freezer

Harvesting your fruit
For freezing fruit should be picked either just before, or when fully ripe. Over-ripe or damaged fruit should not be frozen.

Varieties

Apples	Arthur Turner, Bramley Seedling, Corry's Wonder, Encore, George Neal, Golden Noble, Lane's Prince Albert, Oxford Friend, Sowman's Seedling, Wellington, Wooldbrook Russet. [U.S.: Macoun, McIntosh, Stayman Winesap, Ionared.]
Apricots	Moorpark. [U.S.: Farmingdale, Veecot, Wenatchee, Earlisil.]
Blackberries	Ashton Cross, Himalaya Giant, Merton Early, Oregon Thornless.
Blackcurrants	Baldwin, Boskoop, Laxton's Giant, Malvern's Cross and Blacksmith, Seabrook's Black, Wellington XXX, Westwich Choice.
Cherries	Circassian, Governor Wood, Montmorency, Noir de Guben. [U.S.: Bing, Napoleon.]
Gooseberries	Careless, Golden Drop, Green Gem, Keepsake, Lancer, Leveller. [U.S.: Poorman.]
Loganberries	L.Y. 59
Peaches	Hale's Early (stone-free). [U.S.: Elberta, J. H. Hale, Belle of Georgia, Ris-Oso Gem, Stark's Early.]
Pears	Burre Bedford, Clapp's Favourite, Doyenne du Comice, Gorham, Louise Bonne, Williams' Bon Cretien. [U.S.: Bartlett, Colett, Max-Red, Seckel.]
Plums	Apricot Gage, Belle de Louvain, Cambridge Gage, Count Althann's Gage, Greengage, Jefferson's Gage, Oullin's Gage, Shropshire Prune Damson, Victoria, Warwickshire Drooper, Yellow Egg. [U.S.: Starley, Santa Rosa, Miracle, Burbank Elephant Heart.]
Raspberries	Early Red, Exploit Jewel, Glen Clova, Lloyd George, Malling Enterprise, Malling Jewel, Norfolk Giant, Phyllis King, Promise, September Wellington. [U.S.: Fallgold, Canby, Sodus, Black Hawk, Willamette.]
Redcurrants	Laxten No. 1, Red Lake. [U.S.: Wilder.]
Rhubarb	Champagne, Glaskin's Perpetual, Linnaeus, The Sutton, Timporley Early, Victoria. [U.S.: Valentine, Canada Red.]
Strawberries	Cambridge Favourite, Cambridge Late Pine, Cambridge Prizewinner, Cambridge Rival, Cambridge Vigour, Gorella, Talisman, Templar Royal Sovereign. [U.S.: Fairfax, Fresno, Florida Ninety, Puget Beauty.]

Above and below: Gooseberries which are to be cooked should be picked before they soften.

Left: The season for eating cherries is all too brief. Freezing is the best way to preserve them for any length of time.

Herbs to grow for your freezer

Most common herbs freeze very well. This means you can store fresh herbs for use during the winter months. Freezing gives more satisfactory results than traditional drying as freezing retains the subtle flavour of the herbs.

Freeze herbs free-flow on a tray. When firm, pack in polythene [plastic] bags, seal and label. While frozen, roll a rolling pin over the polythene [plastic] bag and the brittle herbs will shatter. It will save you the laborious job of chopping the herbs at a later date.

Left: Parsley is one of the most useful herbs. It can be chopped and sprinkled over nearly every savoury dish.
Right: A selection of herbs drying in small bunches in the kitchen.

VARIETIES	SOWING	USES
Parsley	Sow annually from March onwards in rows 30 cm (12 inches) apart. Thin seedlings to 15 cm (6 inches). Seeds should be soaked overnight in hot water before sowing.	Frozen parsley can be stored for several months in the freezer and is best used in cooking as it tends to go limp on defrosting. However, frozen sprigs of parsley can be used as a garnish for fish and meat dishes.
Thyme	Sow in early summer in open ground in a sunny dry place.	Thyme is particularly good used with vegetables and rich foods such as shellfish and pork.
Sage	Sow in early summer in a light soil and in a sunny position. Bushes should be cut back each year after flowering.	Sage forms the basis of the classic stuffing for duck, goose and other fatty meats and can be used sparingly in other savoury stuffings.
Chives	Sow from March to July and thin to 30 cm (12 inches) apart. If leaves are picked regularly the plants will grow for years.	Chopped chives add a mild onion flavour to egg, cheese and potato dishes. They make a delicious change to soups and salads.
Marjoram	Sow in early summer and thin seedlings out to 30 cm (12 inches) apart.	Use in poultry, meat, fish and vegetable dishes.
Dill	Sow in a well-drained sunny position. It should be thinned out frequently.	Excellent with all fish dishes, potatoes, cucumber, salads, sauces and pickles.
Rosemary	Sow in early summer in a sheltered place, as a severe frost could kill the bush.	Delicious with roast lamb, kebabs and barbeques.
Mint	Mint cannot readily be grown from seed. It must be grown from root division. Once planted mint grows easily. It prefers a moist spot and some shade.	Mint is often used when cooking new potatoes and peas. But add to a glass of iced tea or chilled white wine to make a refreshing summer drink.

INDEX

Oven Temperatures

	Centigrade	Gas	Fahrenheit
Very cool	130°C	Gas Mark ½	250°F
	140°C	Gas Mark 1	275°F
Cool	150°C	Gas Mark 2	300°F
Warm	170°C	Gas Mark 3	325°F
Moderate	180°F	Gas Mark 4	350°F
Fairly hot	190°C	Gas Mark 5	375°F
	200°C	Gas Mark 6	400°F
Hot	220°C	Gas Mark 7	425°F
Very hot	230°C	Gas Mark 8	450°F
	240°C	Gas Mark 9	475°F
	250°C	Gas Mark 10	500°F

PICTURE CREDITS

Bryce Atwell: 18;
Rex Bamber: 53
Theo Bergstrom: 49;
Steve Bicknell: 64;
Camera Press: 37, 40, 54;
R. J. Corbin: 63
Alan Duns 21, 41, 43, 44 50/1, 54/5, 58
V. Finnis: 64
Melvin Grey: 31, 45, 47
Paul Kemp: 38, 63
Don Last: 17, 20, 23, 25, 29, 34, 39, 48
Michael Leale: 19
David Meldrum: 28
Roger Phillips: 26, 32, 35, 38, 42, 46, 53, 56, 59
The Picture Library: 26
Picturepoint: 61
Iain Reid: 22, 30, 34, 51
David Smith: 49
H. Smith: 61, 63
By Courtesy of Thorn Domestic Appliances